ANGLO CONCERTINA

In the Harmonic Style

Gary Coover

Rollston Press

Anglo Concertina in the Harmonic Style
by Gary Coover

All rights reserved. No part of this book may be reproduced, scanned, transmitted or distributed in any printed or electronic form without the prior permission of the author except in the case of brief quotations embodied in articles or reviews.

Copyright © 2013 Gary Coover

ISBN-13: 978-0615747354
ISBN-10: 0615747353

All arrangements and transcriptions by Gary Coover unless otherwise noted

All tunes are in the public domain unless otherwise noted.

Front Cover Photo: Gremlin 30-button Anglo concertina, c. 1980
Back Cover Photo: Jeffries 30-button Anglo concertina, c. 1900

ROLLSTON PRESS
1717 Ala Wai Boulevard, Suite 1730
Honolulu, HI 96815
USA
www.rollstonpress.com

TABLE OF CONTENTS

INTRODUCTION 5

KEYBOARD 7

TABLATURE 8

MUSICAL NOTES 9

SCALES 11

CHORDS 12

THE THIRD ROW 18

PRACTICE & PERFORMANCE 19

TUNES
- Oh! Susanna 20
- Shepherd's Hey 24
- Ned of the Hill 26
- The Beaver 27
- Waltz Across Texas 28
- Young Collins 29
- Hard Times Come Again No More 30
- Rigs of Marlow 32
- Auld Lang Syne 33
- Herrington Hall 34
- You Are All I Have 35
- Winster Processional 36
- Leaping Jack 37
- Bobbing Joe 38
- The Ash Grove 39
- Parson's Farewell 40
- Michael Turner's Waltz 42
- Country Gardens 44
- The Moon Knows My Heart 45
- Newcastle 46
- Will Kipper's Waltz 47
- For Ireland I'd Not Tell Her Name 48
- The Old & Lost Hornpipe 50
- Fruits & Flowers 52
- Greensleeves 53
- The Minstrel Boy 54
- Burchard's Hornpipe 55
- Kennington Jig 60

PERFORMER SHOWCASE

William Kimber 63
    Country Gardens
John Kirkpatrick 64
    Fair Play
    King George III's Minuet
    The Charabanc Schottische
    Hanged I Shall Be
    Petal of Spice
Jody Kruskal 70
    Fly Around My Pretty Little Miss
    Elk River Blues
Bertram Levy 73
    Bride's March
    New Rigged Ship
Father Kenneth N.J. Loveless 76
    Nutting Girl
Brian Peters 78
    Nymph
    Sweet Sorrow
    Adieu My Lovely Nancy
    Accordion Tune
Andy Turner 83
    Swaggering Boney
    Packington's Pound
    Old Molly Oxford
    Eastwell Park
John Watcham 88
    Monck's March
    Black Joker
    Cuckoo's Nest
    Lumps of Plum Pudding
    Fieldtown Processional

POP, BLUES & CLASSICAL

St. James Infirmary 96
Poor Orphan (Armes Waisenkind) 97
Trumpet Tune in D (by Jeremiah Clarke) 98
The Song from Moulin Rouge 99
Over the Rainbow (from "The Wizard of Oz") 100
Star Spangled Banner (by James Hewitt) 101
In Plenty and In Time of Need (Barbados National Anthem) 104
Pomp & Circumstance (Land of Hope and Glory) 106

ALPHABETICAL LIST OF TUNES 107

THE AUTHOR / ACKNOWLEDGMENTS 108

INTRODUCTION

Although there are many instruments called "concertina" with many different fingering systems and button arrangements, this tutor is specifically written for Anglo concertina – the only type of concertina that plays a different note depending on whether you are pushing or pulling on it.

Instead of the single-note style of playing common to Irish traditional music, this tutor is designed to teach harmonic playing and chords in the more "English" style of playing the Anglo concertina where the melody is played mostly on the right hand side with accompaniment on the left hand side.

This book is written for the 30-button Anglo in the key of C/G, and includes an easy tablature system that can also be used to play tunes on Anglo concertinas in other home keys.

The 20-button "German" concertina consists of two rows of buttons, one in the key of C and one in the key of G. The 30-button "Anglo-German" concertina has an extra third row on top with additional notes and accidentals. The most common arrangement of the top row is the one used by the Wheatstone and Lachenal concertina companies throughout the 1800's and 1900's.

Concertinas with Jeffries accidentals will be identical on the left hand side to the Wheatstone/Lachenal 30-button instrument, but 8 out of 10 notes on the right hand side top row will be different. This will not affect the left hand chords as shown in this tutor, but might require some adjustments and additional dexterity to play the melodies correctly (or close enough).

One of the unique aspects of the Anglo concertina is that no two people play it exactly the same way. There are as many styles of playing as there are players and instruments, and in celebration of that fact this book presents transcriptions of tunes played by some of the top players in the world today so you can learn and appreciate their style on the way to creating your own.

Many of the tunes transcribed here were originally recorded on concertinas with additional buttons and with notes not available on the standard 30-button layout. Luckily, only a few minor adjustments here and there were needed to make the tunes work. If you have the extra buttons by all means learn to use them, but every tune in this tutor can be played successfully on an Anglo concertina with only 30-buttons.

For the beginner, this tutor will teach you some simple tunes and show you the basic notes and patterns to play tunes and create chords using an easily understandable tablature system.

For the intermediate player this tutor will help you get away from playing just along the rows by teaching cross-row techniques that will increase your note and phrasing possibilities.

For the advanced player, this tutor provides several challenging tunes plus note-for-note transcriptions of tunes recorded by well-known Anglo players.

The Anglo concertina is much more than just "two harmonicas tied together" – it has a quirky yet robust arrangement of notes, not unlike that of a typewriter, that can be mastered to play an amazing variety of tunes. This book will help you do just that.

The tablature and transcriptions presented in this tutor should be considered as guidelines that are an example of one way to play the tune, and are just frameworks for you to build upon. Professional performers often vary notes and chords, add ornaments, flourishes, and do various things to make the tune more interesting with each repetition, and so can you.

Don't be afraid to experiment on your own with extra notes, harmonies, chords, ornamentations and twiddly bits. At worst you might get an awful clanger, and at best you might discover a fantastic variation that you can incorporate into your version of the tune. If you think a different chord works better, then use it! Feel free to use alternate buttons to make a phrase smoother or more bouncy. Once again, the tablature just shows one way of playing the tune, not the only way.

Notation of which finger to use on which button has been purposefully avoided, since everyone has different size hands and different ways of holding and playing the instrument. The layout of the Anglo makes it pretty obvious which fingering to use most of the time. The rest of the time, I trust you can figure out what works best for you. It's not always obvious and sometimes might involve some tricky stretches, playing two notes with one finger or jumping quickly from note to note, but don't give up just because it's hard to do. Some of the best tunes have awkward fingerings that just take practice to make perfect.

The tunes in this tutor start out very easy but get difficult fairly quickly, especially if you are accustomed to just playing along one row. Playing across the rows and utilizing the third row on top are essential for learning how to play the Anglo in the full harmonic style. All of your fingers will get a good workout, including the pinkies on both hands.

Just remember that not all tunes or all types of music can be played on the Anglo. It has serious limitations that prevent certain phrases and chords from ever happening. Although the Anglo is theoretically chromatic, you don't always have all the notes you might want in the same direction for playing both melody and chords. No matter how hard you may try, you simply cannot play one note on the push while simultaneously playing another on the pull!

But within the Anglo's many limitations and restrictions is a structure that can be mastered to play a lot more music than most people think is possible. The hope is that this book will help you realize the full potential of your instrument and the person playing it.

If you're like me, you probably hate scales and exercises, so this book is going to teach you lots of tunes instead. So, hide the case in a closet, leave your concertina out where you'll pick it up and play it more and more every day, and enjoy your voyage of discovery!

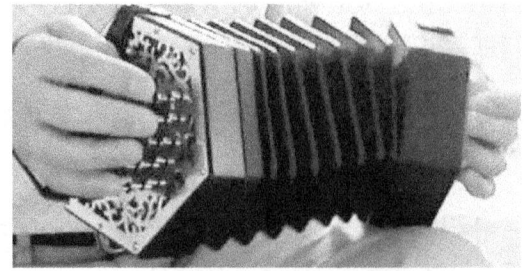

KEYBOARD

The buttons and corresponding notes on the 30-button C/G Anglo concertina are arranged in a somewhat logical system. The middle row is basically all notes in the key of C and the bottom row is all notes in the key of G. The top row has alternate notes plus extra sharps and flats. Notes lower in pitch are on the left side of the instrument and higher notes are on the right. In this graphic the notes shown on top of the line are on the push, notes shown below the line are on the pull. Standard abc notation has been used to show the pitches of the notes.

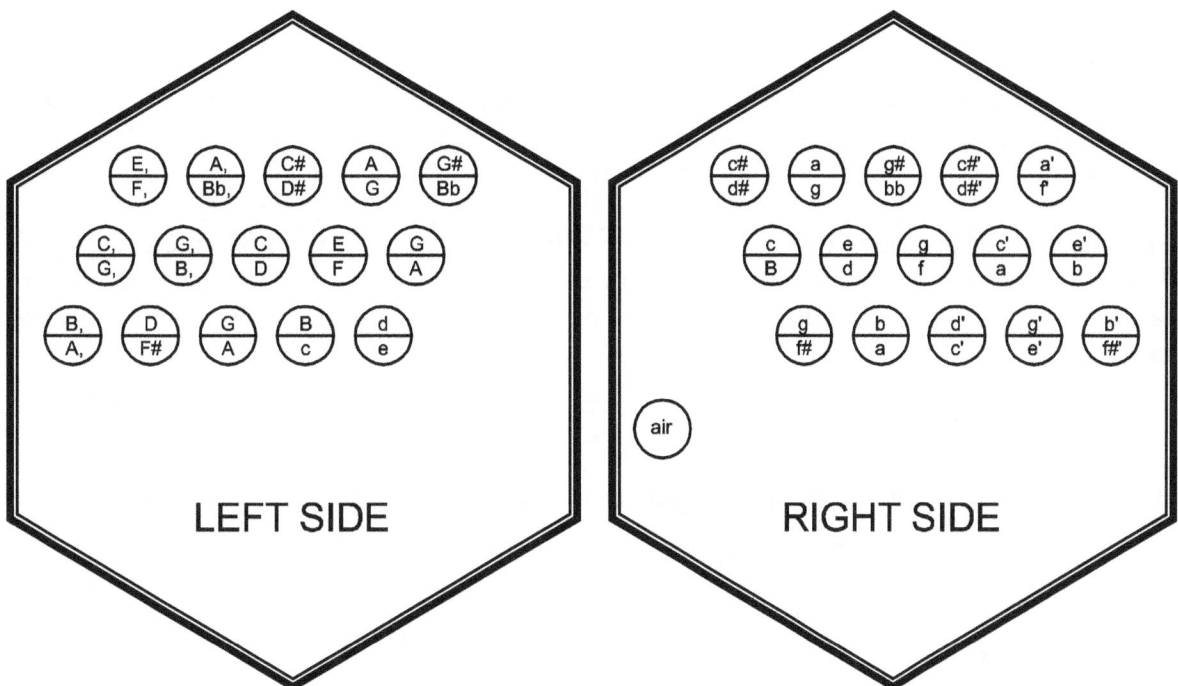

And here is the button numbering system used for the tablature in this tutor:

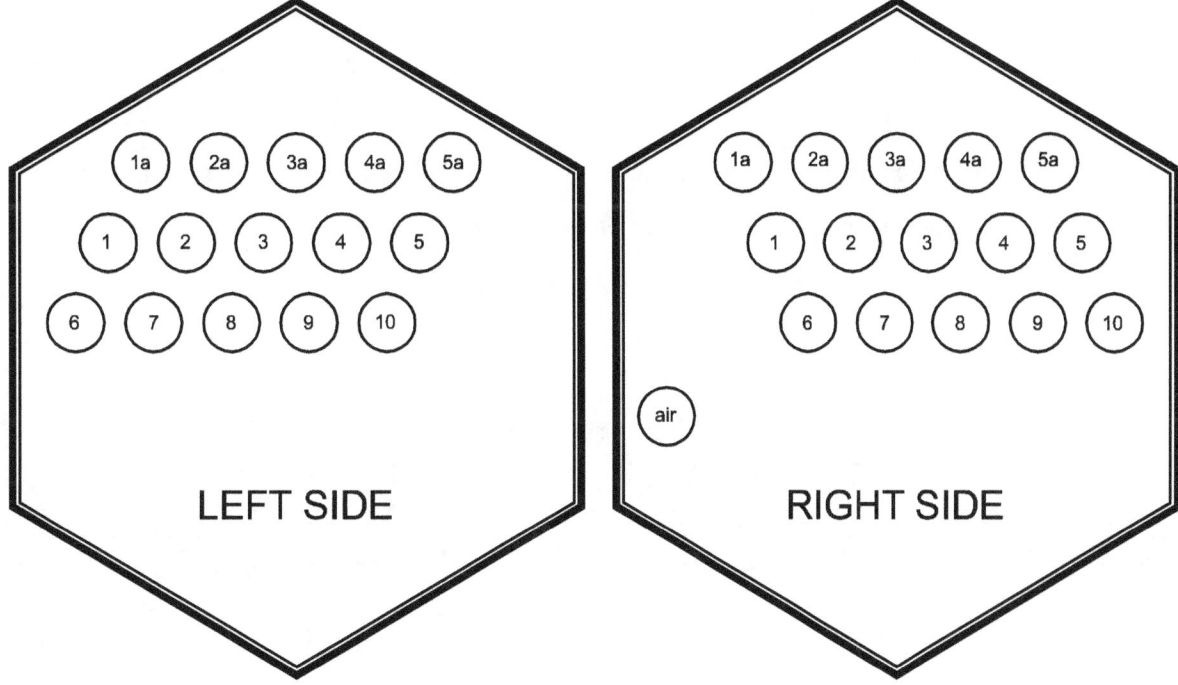

Anglo Concertina in the Harmonic Style

TABLATURE

Regardless of whether you can read music of not, this tablature system can be applied to Anglo concertinas in the key of C/G and to Anglo concertinas in any other combination of keys.

There are almost as many numbering and tablature systems out there as there are buttons on the Anglo concertina, and although many appear logical and have been developed with much effort, most are very difficult for the beginner to understand quickly. It seems the very nature of the Anglo having two notes in different directions for each button and sometimes having alternate notes on other buttons encourages this confusion.

The button numbering system utilized in this book is easy to grasp, also works for 20-button instruments, and is the same system used by the early German concertina makers in the 1870's as well as by Chris Sherburn, Jody Kruskal, Dan Worrall and many others.

The tablature in this book differs from all other tutors in the indication of bellows direction. Most indicate push or pull (in/out, press/draw etc.) using characters (^), letters (P, D), dots (.) or a host of other symbols. As visually confusing as many of these are, they might as well just use "P" for push and "P" for pull!

How the tablature works in this book:

- The buttons are numbered using the "1a-10" numbering system for each side.
- Buttons on the right hand side are shown above the musical notes.
- Buttons on the left hand side are shown below the musical notes.
- Notes on the push are shown by button number only.
- Notes on the pull are shown by button number with a line across the top. Long phrases all on the pull will have one long continuous line above the button numbers.
- Notes that are held for a longer period of time are indicated with dashed lines after the button number.
- An "x" indicates no accompaniment note is to be played on that particular beat.
- Alternate fingerings are shown in parentheses.
- Chord symbols are shown at the top of each line of music.

EXAMPLE:

MUSICAL NOTES

For those of you who read music and/or abc notation, here are the buttons and the notes:

KEYBOARD LAYOUT - abc notation

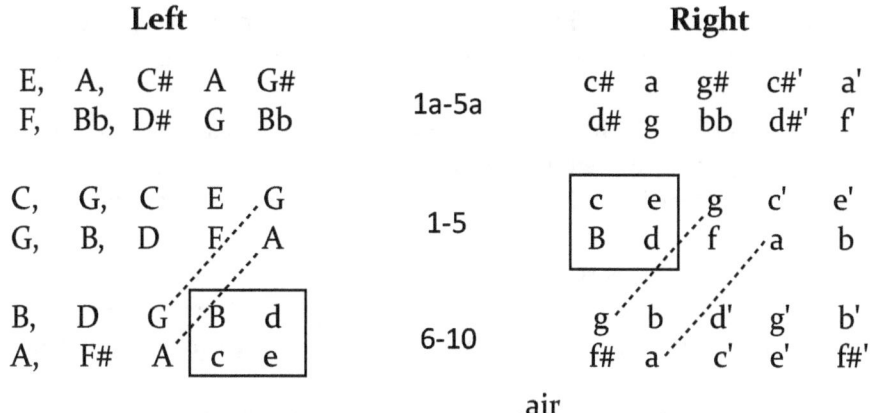

Four notes overlap, but in different directions: #9 & #10 on the left, and #1 & #2 on the right.

And four buttons have exact duplicates in the same direction: #5/#8 on the push (G) and #5/#8 on the pull (A) on the left side, and #3/#6 on the push (g) and #4/#7 on the pull (a) on the right side. You can use them interchangeably depending on which fingering works best.

For harmonic accompaniment, it's a good thing that some notes have duplicates even if they are sometimes in different directions, sometimes in the same direction, and sometimes on different sides. The notes you only have in one place in one direction will be the tricky ones.

Although the Anglo concertina is theoretically chromatic, that only applies to single notes being played one at a time. You will quickly discover the amount of chromatic-ness depends on the tunes and chords you are playing, whether you are pushing or pulling, and which key you are in.

The thing that will vex you most about playing the Anglo is the fact that certain fairly important notes occur in one direction only. Depending on what keys you play in and how fancy you make your arrangements, these notes will often control how you structure your melody and chords:

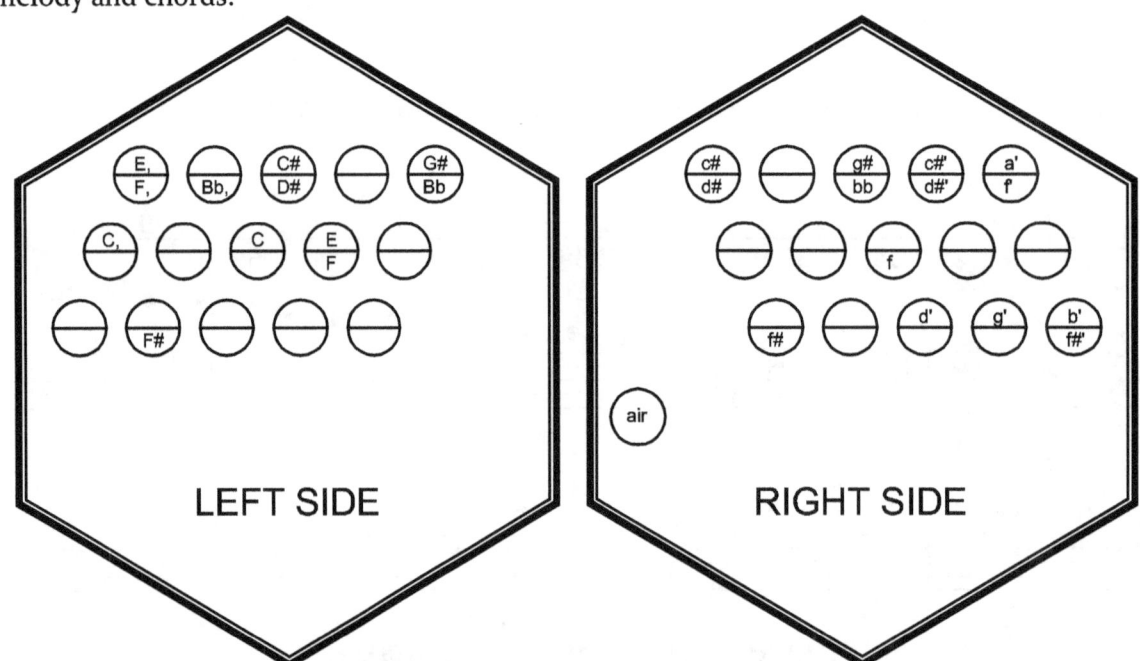

For playing both melody and chords at the same time, you won't always have all the notes you might want in the same direction. This is the biggest limitation of the 30-button Anglo, and it is something that must be acknowledged, dealt with, and often worked around.

But it doesn't make it impossible, just a little more problematic, especially if you are wanting to use complex chords in your arrangements. Luckily, you do not have to play every note of every chord every time – sometimes just a few notes can suggest the chord you want.

On the right hand side, the notes that will drive you the craziest will be the "f" in the middle row, and the "f#" and "d'" on the bottom row. Add the "c#" on the top row if you're playing in the key of D. You've only got these notes in one place and in one direction. Period.

The same goes for the left hand side, where you've only got the one "F#" on the bottom row, the "C", "E" and "F" on the middle row, and "E,", "F," and "C#" on the top row. The lack of a low "D," can also be frustrating.

Certain keys work really well on the Anglo, others less so or not at all. You'll find C, G, F and Dm work best. Transposing to a key that fits the instrument better is a very common occurrence. You just have to work with the buttons and notes in the directions that you've got.

SCALES

To help you get familiar with how the notes go together with the pushing and pulling of the bellows, here are some major scales in various keys showing all notes available for the scale. The big challenge of playing the Anglo is to work around the notes that have no alternates. When you do have alternates they can be invaluable to keep you from running out of air or tying your fingers into knots. Alternates will also allow you to play certain phrases more smoothly.

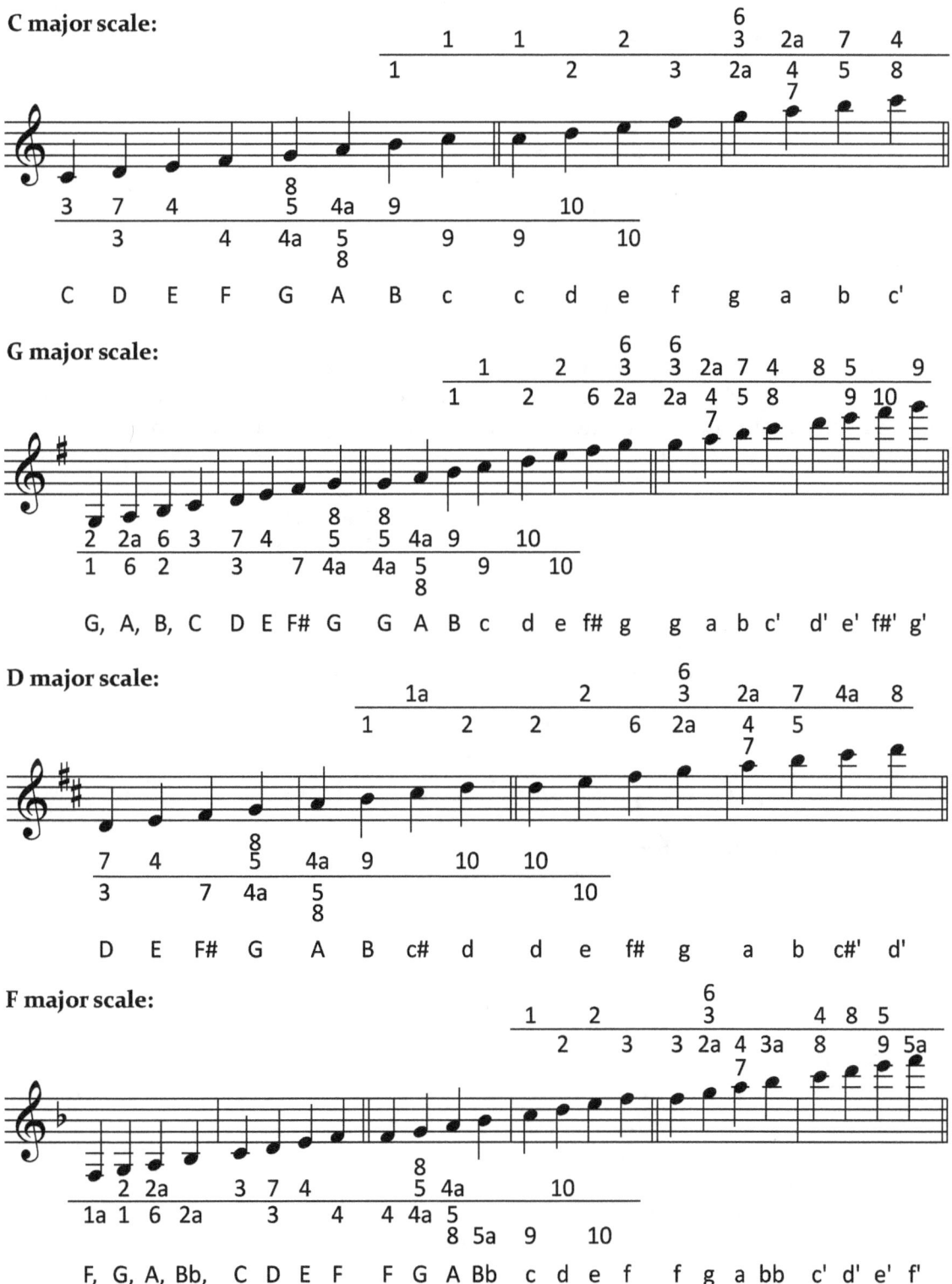

Anglo Concertina in the Harmonic Style

CHORDS

To fully play in the harmonic style, you need to learn basic left hand chords and how to create appropriate accompaniments. The Anglo has no preset chords – it is up to you to find and combine the various notes to get the chords you want. There is a lot of information published already on musical theory, chording and accompaniment, so we will only briefly discuss chords in general.

Chords are created by combining notes in standard musical steps, based on the 7 whole note intervals of the modern scale. The chords used most often in traditional folk music are:

Major chord	1-3-5 (whole steps, not button numbers)
Minor chord	1-3b-5
Modal chord	1-5

Modal chords are very common in traditional folk music. These exact same chords are also known as "power chords" in heavy metal rock music!

There is a famous chord progression known as the "three chord trick": I-IV-V. These three major chords, along with the associated relative minor will work for an amazing number of tunes and songs. Of course there are other fancier chords and variations, but these are the basics:

Key	Chords I-IV-V	Relative Minor (VI)
C	**C-F-G**	**Am**
G	**G-C-D**	**Em**
D	**D-G-A**	**Bm**
F	**F-Bb-C**	**Dm**

The corresponding notes of these chords are:

Chord	Notes
C	CEG
G	GBD
D	DF#A
F	FAC
A	AC#E
Bb	BbDF
Am	ACE
Em	EGB
Bm	BDF#
Dm	DFA

To tie all this to the Anglo concertina, here's what some of the more common chords look like:

	PUSH	PULL	
○○○○ ○○●●● ○○○○	C 3-4-5	Dm 3-4-5	
○○○○○ ○○○○○ ○○●●●	G (2)-8-9-10	Am (6)-8-9-10	
○●○○○ ○○●●○ ○○○○○	Am 2a-3-4	Bb 2a-3-4	
●○○○○ ○○○●● ○○○●○	Em 1a-4-5-9	F 1a-4-5-9	
○●●●● ○○○●○ ○○○○○	A 2a-3a-4		

PULL chords (right side):

	G		Gm
○○○○● ●●●○○ ○○○○○	1-2-3-4a	○○○●● ●○●○○ ○○○○○	1-3-4a-5a

	E		D		C/D#/F#/A dim
●○○○● ○○○●○ ○○○●○	1-4-5a-9	○○○○○ ○○●○● ○●●○○	3-7-8/5	○○●○○ ○○○○○ ○●●●○	3a-7-8-9-R1a

	Bm		B
○○○○○ ○●●○○ ○●○○○	2-3-7	○○●○○ ○●○○○ ○●○○○	2-3a-7

As you can see, some chords work best in certain directions, and sometimes you get two completely different chords with the exact same buttons depending on bellows direction. It will be confusing at first, but will come in quite handy once you get used to it.

Anglo Concertina in the Harmonic Style

Let's practice some of the more common chords and chord progressions:

LEFT HAND – KEY OF C

	Buttons played	Button #	Direction
C	○○○○○ ●○●●● ○○○○○	5 4 3 1	Push
F̄	●○○○○ ○○○●● ○○○●○	9 5 4 1a	Pull
Ḡ	○○○●○ ●○●○○ ○○○○○	4a 3 1	Pull
C	○○○○○ ●○●●● ○○○○○	5 4 3 1	Push

LEFT HAND – KEY OF G

	Buttons played	Button #	Direction
G	○○○○○ ○●○○○ ○○●●●	10 9 8 2	Push
C	○○○○○ ○○●●● ○○○○○	5 4 3	Push
D̄	○○○○○ ○○●○● ○●○○○	5 7 3	Pull
G	○○○○○ ○●○○○ ○○●●●	10 9 8 2	Push

14 Anglo Concertina in the Harmonic Style

LEFT HAND – KEY OF C

Chord	Buttons played	Button #	Direction
C	○○○○○ ○○●●● ○○○○○	5 4 3	Push
Am	○●○○○ ○○●●○ ○○○○○	4 3 2a	Push
F	●○○○○ ○○○●● ○○○●○	9 5 4 1a	Pull
G	○○○●○ ●○●○○ ○○○○○	4a 3 1	Pull

LEFT HAND – KEY OF G

Chord	Buttons played	Button #	Direction
G	○○○○○ ○●○○○ ○○●●●	10 9 8 2	Push
Em	●○○○○ ○○○●● ○○○●○	9 5 4 1a	Push
C	○○○○○ ○○●●● ○○○○○	5 4 3	Push
D	○○○○○ ○○●○● ○●○○○	5 7 3	Pull

You can play the G chord on the push or the pull, depending on the song and the air in the bellows. It's not always easy to balance melody notes, chords, bellows direction and air.

Anglo Concertina in the Harmonic Style

Here are those same chord progressions in tablature, showing the G chord in both directions. Practice these chord transitions until you can move smoothly between each one.

The #2 button has been shown as an alternate in the G chord, since you will probably play the G chord on the pull as #1-3-4a most often. Feel free to add or substitute the #2 button.

Key of C:

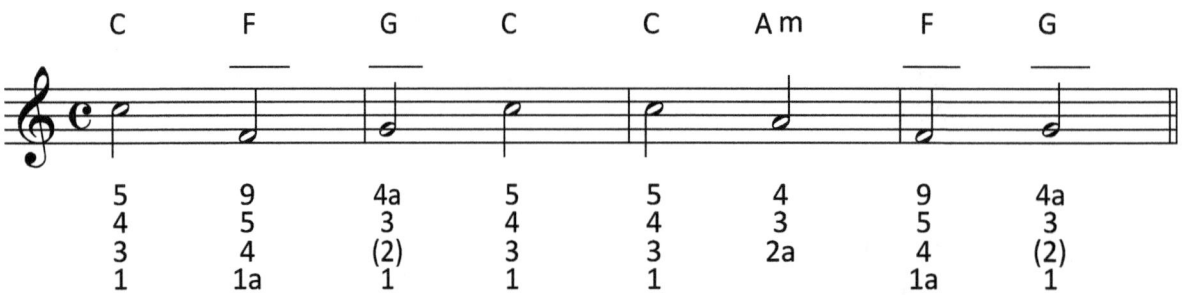

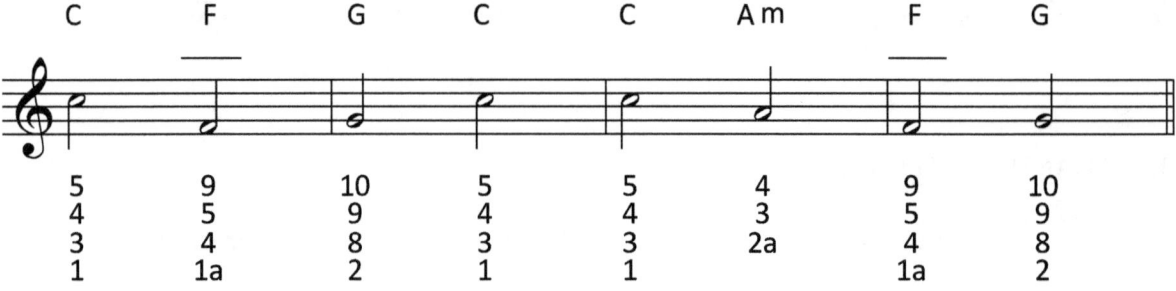

Key of G:

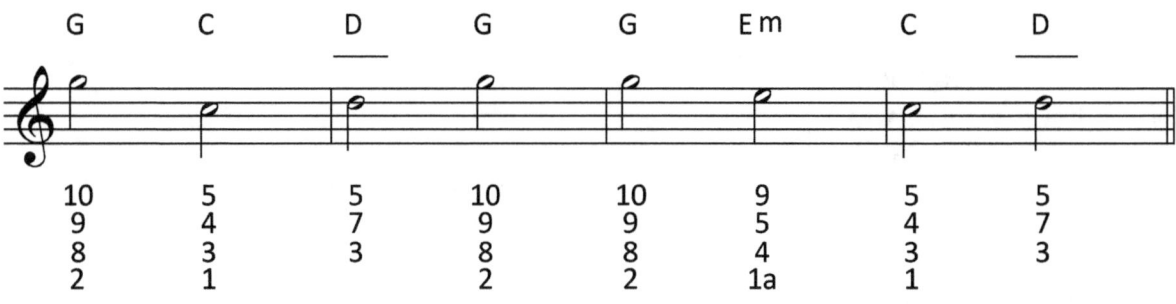

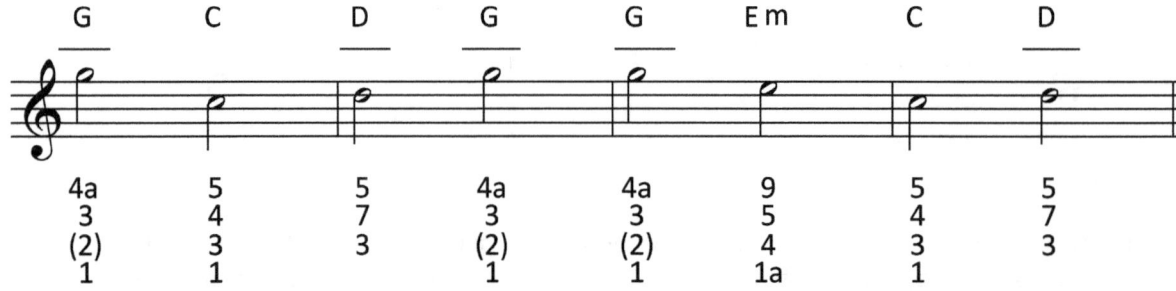

Here are some common "oom-pah" chords and progressions to practice. You can use combinations of these chords to play many accompaniments even if you don't know the melody. And yes, your little finger can eventually be trained to master bass notes and bass runs.

Key of C:
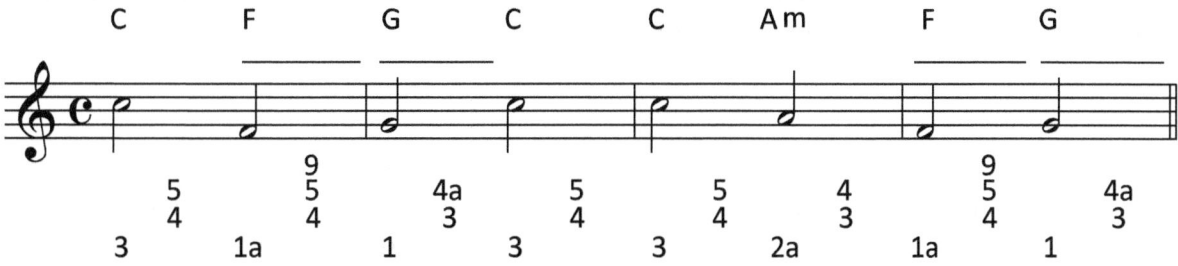

Key of G:
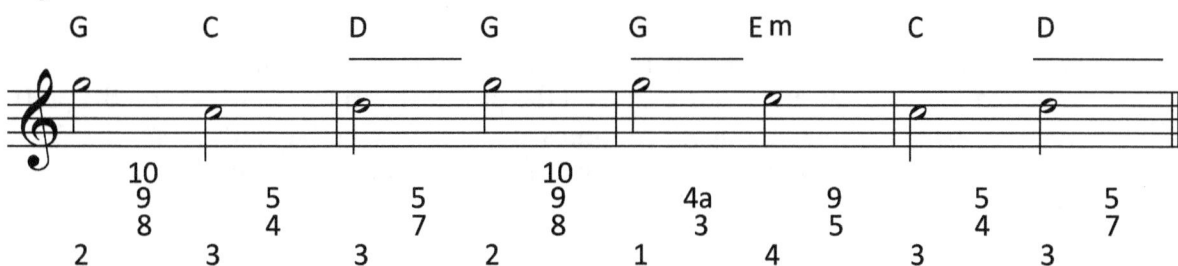

Try these again, interchanging the push or pull G chord.

Key of D:

Key of F:
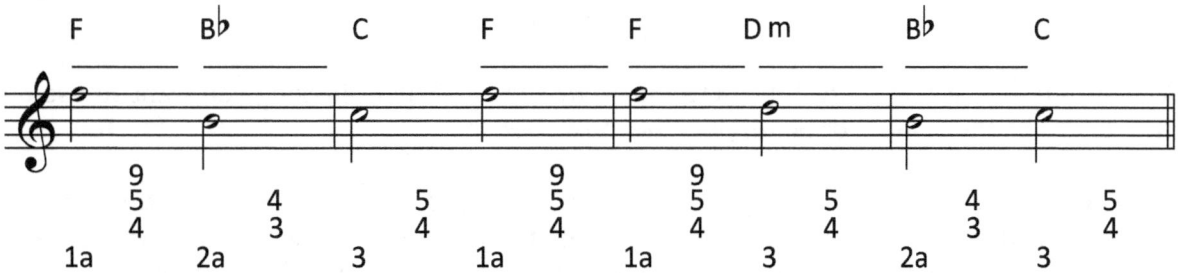

THE THIRD ROW

As you have learned by now, the third row on top is not as scary as it initially seems. As you get more familiar with the keyboard layout you will find the third row has alternate notes that come in very handy plus accidentals you can use to create chromatic runs and complex chords.

Most of the tunes in this tutor make good use of the third row. Here is a brief explanation of the buttons and when they are most used:

Left Hand Side:

1a	E/F	**Often** (push for E and Em chords), **Often** (pull for F chord)
2a	A/Bb	**Often** (push for A and Am chords), Seldom (pull for Bb chord)
3a	C#/D#	Seldom (push for A chord), Seldom (pull for diminished chord)
4a	A/G	**Often** (push for A and Am chords), **Often** (pull for G chord)
5a	G#/Bb	Seldom (push for E chord), Seldom (pull for Bb chord)

Right Hand Side:

1a	C#/D#	Seldom (mostly for tunes in key of D on the push)
2a	A/G	**Often** (tunes with A on the push), **Often** (tunes with G on the pull)
3a	G#/Bb	Seldom (mostly for tunes in key of Dm on the pull)
4a	C#/D#	Seldom (mostly for tunes in key of D or A on the push)
5a	A/F	Seldom (very high and squeaky)

See, it's not so bad. Only 4 out of 10 (shown in bold) are used with any great frequency.

A major advantage of the notes on the third row is providing alternate buttons in different directions which can be very useful in phrasing as well as chord creation.

Here is an example of some triplets on the right hand side that can be played with or without the third row buttons:

3 - 4̄ - 3	push/pull/push
3 - 2a - 3	push/push/push (all push)
3̄ - 3 - 3̄	pull/push/pull
3̄ - 2̄a - 3̄	pull/pull/pull (all pull)

When to use either option will be determined by the particular phrasing you want to use on the tune, whether smooth or bouncy fits the music best.

Now that we've talked about the C-row, G-row and Top/Third row, try to not think of the Anglo in terms of rows. Treat it more like you would a typewriter where you learn patterns and locations of particular notes that can be found in anywhere on any row or either end.

PRACTICE & PERFORMANCE

Notes are not music. Tablature is not music. Pushing buttons is not music.

"Music" is your personal expression that you create from all these elementary pieces. Of course you need to learn the basic buttons, directions, notes and alternates, but then you need to study original recordings if possible and then work to develop your own interpretations.

If you are one of those people who think playing everything blazingly fast is impressive, it's not. You'll end up butchering the tune, losing any sense of music, and will truly look like a total idiot to anyone who knows better. Every tune will have at least one tempo that makes it particularly musical and enjoyable to dance to or listen to – use your ears and your heart to find that tempo.

Some suggestions for practicing and finding your style:

1. Listen to the tune obsessively until you can hum or sing the melody.

2. Play along with an original recording if possible. Use a computer program like "The Amazing Slow Downer®" if you need to slow it down until you can play it up to speed.

3. Give difficult sections the "5 Minute Test" – loop and repeat for a solid 5 minutes.

4. Don't worry too much about running out of air until you can play it up to tempo.

5. Don't practice every day – hit it hard and then give it a few days rest from time to time.

6. Try playing slowly and deliberately, try playing insanely fast.

7. Try playing every note very staccato, try playing every note very quietly.

8. Try playing with exaggerated drama and emphasis, work the bellows.

9. Don't let the accompaniment bury the melody.

10. Play the whole tune delicately and sensitively instead of forcefully and loudly.

11. Memorize your playing by weaning yourself from the music and the tablature.

12. Record yourself and listen to the playback. Is what you just played something you (or anyone else) would want to listen to? If not, keep practicing and fine-tuning.

And last but not least, watch yourself in a mirror or webcam to make sure you're not a zombie with "concertina face", and that you're not breathing in and out the same time as the bellows.

Once you've learned the tune you will need to play it over and over and over until your fingers and your subconscious know exactly where to go and what to do. Motor skills and muscle memory take <u>weeks</u> of practice and repetition, but persevere and you will have the tune forever.

When you get to the point where you can comfortably play in front of others, you've made it!

TUNES

Let's start with an easy well-known tune that can be played on just three buttons. This is a minstrel show tune written by Stephen Foster in 1847. The melody can be played with three buttons on the left hand side: #3, #4 & #5 (starting with middle C in the middle of the C-row).

LEFT HAND ONLY

Oh! Susanna

Stephen Foster

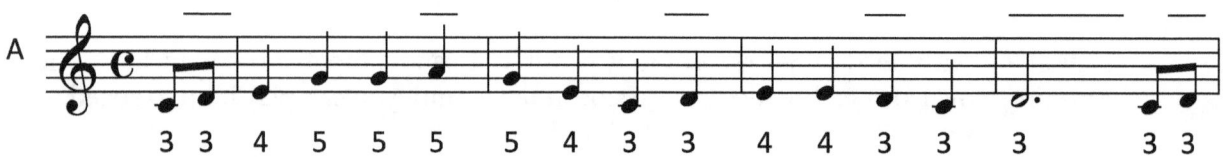

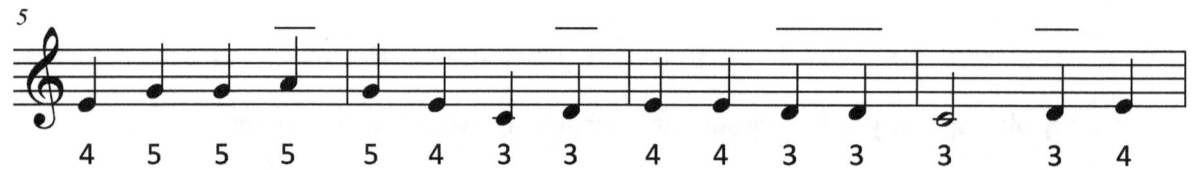

Anglo Concertina in the Harmonic Style

You can also play it on the right hand side with only 4 buttons on the middle row (#1,#2,#3 & #4).

RIGHT HAND ONLY

Buttons played

Oh! Susanna

Stephen Foster

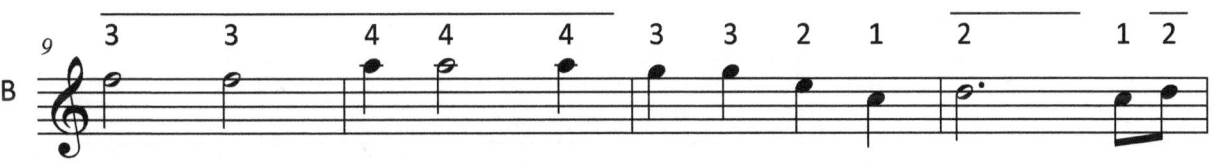

Anglo Concertina in the Harmonic Style

A technique utilized by many old time Anglo players is to play in octaves. This gives a lot more volume to the melody and has the added benefit of not conflicting with any accompaniment or chords from other instruments.

Since the middle and bottom row scales of the Anglo have 3 notes pushing and 4 notes pulling for a complete 7-note scale, octave playing is not as easy as it seems since there is a natural jog in the note sequence that has to be accounted for as you go up and down the scale.

OCTAVES – BOTH HANDS

Buttons played

Oh! Susanna

Stephen Foster

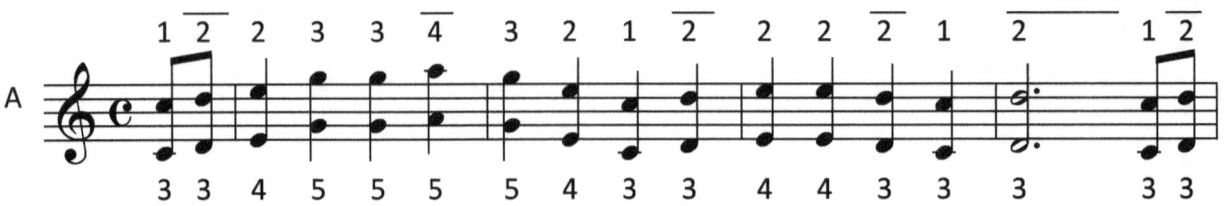

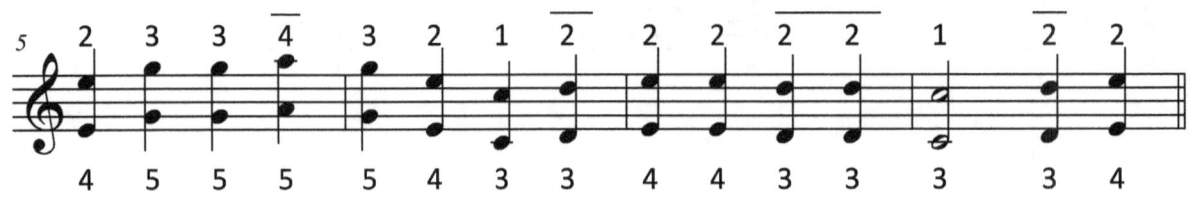

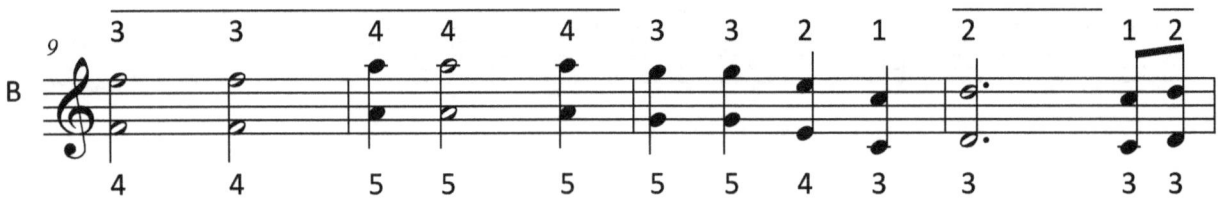

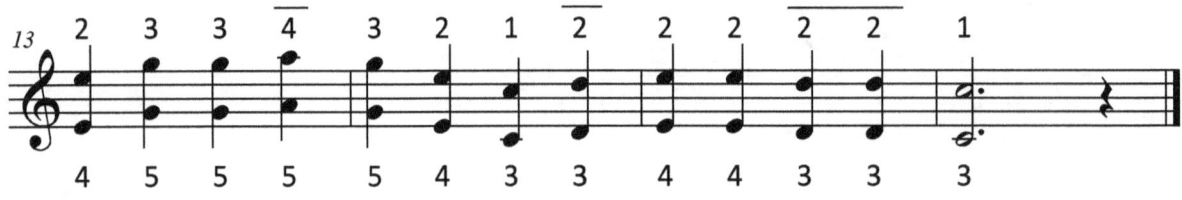

Anglo Concertina in the Harmonic Style

Here is the world's easiest harmony – just play the button to the left of every melody note, push or pull. You'll be amazed how often it works, and it's a lot easier than it looks. This is one of the beauties of the Anglo – adjacent notes are often compatible harmonies.

HARMONY – LEFT HAND

Buttons played

Oh! Susanna

Stephen Foster

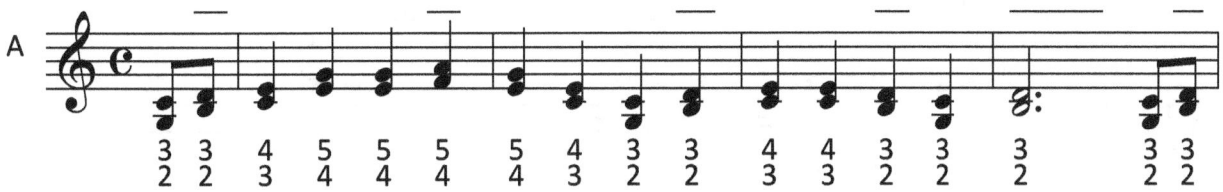

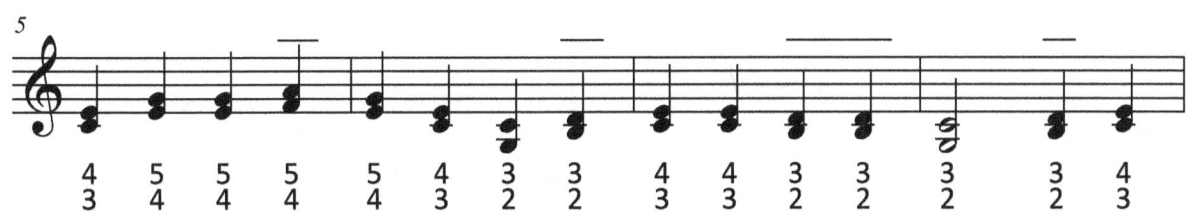

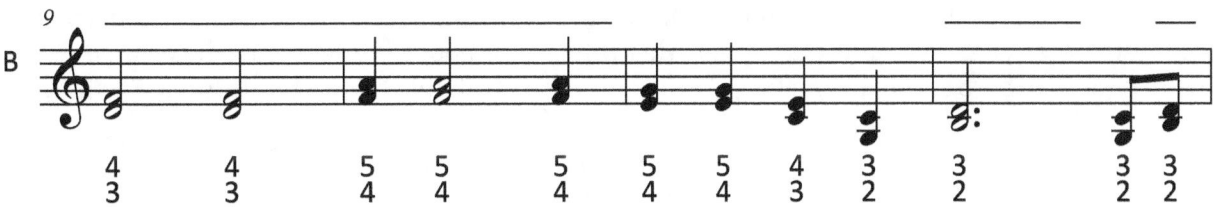

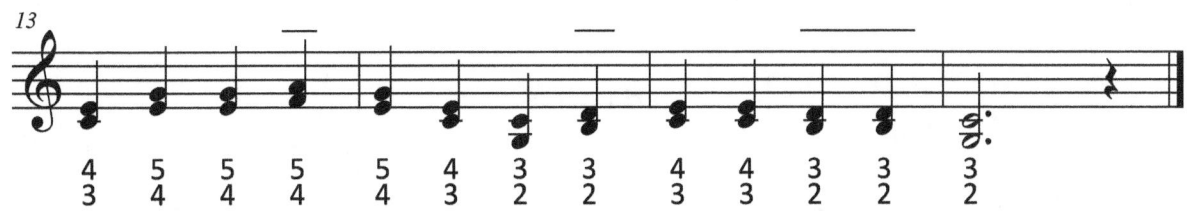

You can also play this on the bottom row in the key of G just as easily as on the middle row in the key of C. Try to play every note crisply and cleanly.

Anglo Concertina in the Harmonic Style

Shepherd's Hey is an old traditional English Morris dance tune from the village of Bampton in Oxfordshire, England. The entire melody can be played with only 3 buttons on the right hand side.

RIGHT HAND ONLY

Shepherd's Hey

traditional English

A single note melody is all well and good, but the Anglo also has the capability of playing multiple notes at a time, and that's what this tutor is all about. So let's introduce some left hand chords to accompany the melody. We'll start off with simple block chords for C, F and G.

LH Chords

Shepherd's Hey

Now here's a way to play those same chords a little more interestingly:

Shepherd's Hey

Sounds much better doesn't it? So much for basic training, let's move on to more tunes.

Here's a lovely Irish slow air called "Éamonn an Chnoic" in Irish Gaelic, which is known in English as "Ned of the Hill". This arrangement is very easy to play and is proof you don't need a lot of notes and chords to make something very beautiful.

Buttons played

Ned of the Hill

traditional Irish

Arranged for concertina by Molly Bennett, used by permission.

This tune comes from a 1770's manuscript found in Lincoln, England. Called "The Beaver", it is named after the flat-topped hats that were once quite the fashion in England.

Buttons played

The Beaver

traditional English, as played by Liam Robinson

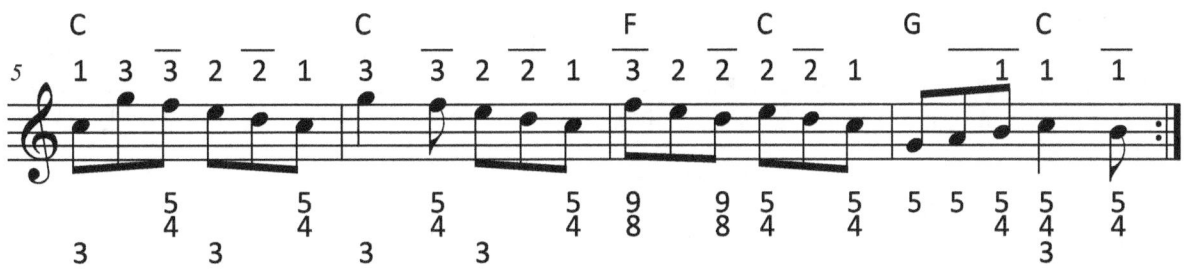

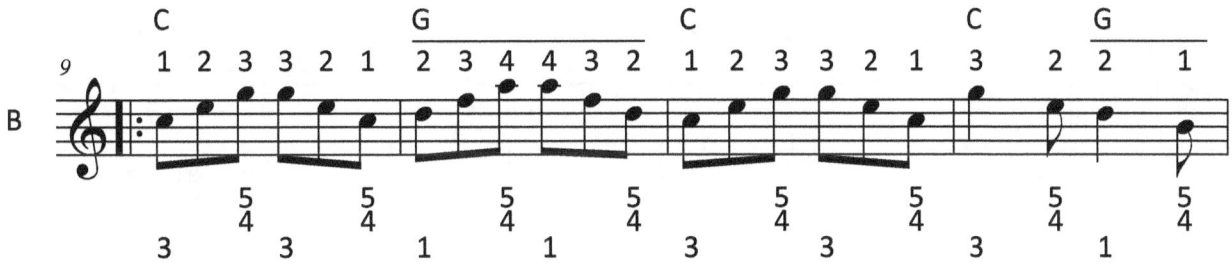

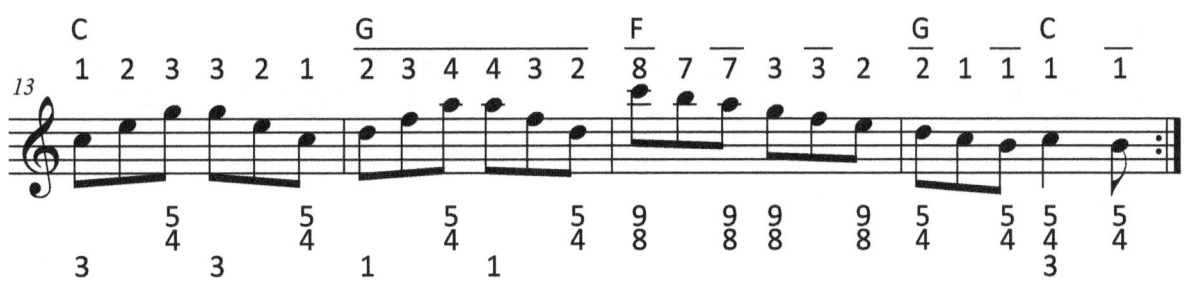

Anglo Concertina in the Harmonic Style

Waltzes are a good way to practice "oom-pah" chords. The arrangement of this classic Country & Western song comes from the playing and teaching of Jody Kruskal.

Buttons played

Waltz Across Texas

Q.T. Tubb
Arranged for Anglo concertina by Jody Kruskal

Copyright © 1965 Ernest Tubb Music, used by permission

From the village of Bledington in Gloucestershire, England, this tune accompanies a traditional Morris dance performed by six dancers with ribbons, bells and long sticks.

Buttons played

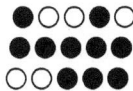
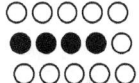

Young Collins
(Bledington)

traditional English

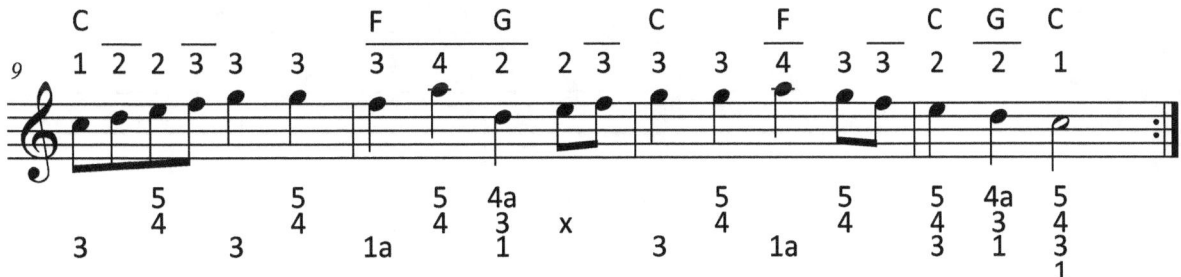

Anglo Concertina in the Harmonic Style

Here's another Stephen Foster song, first published in 1854. Play it slowly and with lots of emotion – keep in mind the first line of the song: "Let us pause in life's pleasures and count its many tears".

Buttons played

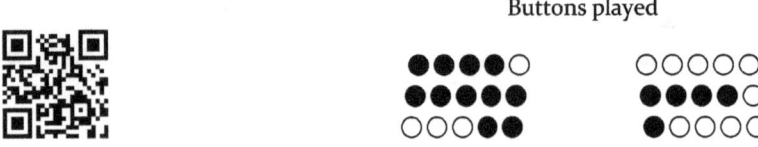

Hard Times Come Again No More

Stephen Foster

Hard Times Come Again No More (cont.)

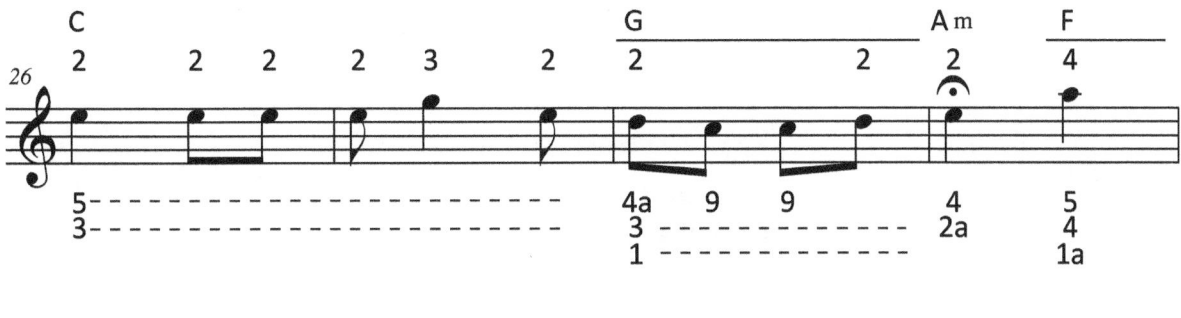

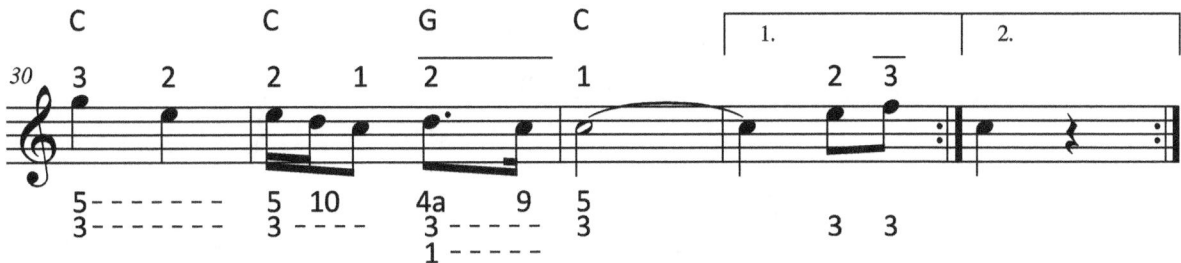

As you have discovered with many of these tunes, the melody is not always played on just the middle row. To fully play the Anglo concertina in the harmonic style you will often be playing melodies on all three rows. Don't panic, this tutor will help you get familiar with all the notes used most often, wherever they are found.

And you'll notice in many cases that the melody is not entirely on the right hand side – it's perfectly ok to pick up melody notes on the left hand side when you need to.

Measure 17 of this tune is a good example of an "underhanded" left hand fingering trick that you need to be comfortable with to play more smoothly in the harmonic style. With your little finger on button #2 and your middle finger on button #4a, hold steady and reach under with your ring finger to play the melody note on button #9.

The Anglo concertina is a unique arrangement of individual notes, two for each button, with lower notes mostly on the left and higher notes mostly on the right. Depending on the melody and chords you are playing, the notes you need could be anywhere on the instrument. Maybe even in several places at once. And maybe not always terribly easy to get to. That's the frustration and the beauty of the Anglo.

Similar to the Irish song and polka "Rakes of Mallow", this tune is called "Rigs of Marlow" and is for a traditional Morris dance from the village of Headington Quarry near Oxford, England. The dance is a stick dance and the accented chords in the "B" part coincide with clashing of the sticks. An alternate bass line of notes only is shown in parentheses in the "A" part.

Buttons played

Rigs of Marlow
(Headington)

traditional English, as played by John Watcham

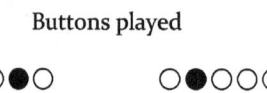

From the Ashley Hutchings CD "Son of Morris On" and
the Albion Morris CD "Still Dancing After All These Years"

Here's your chance to mimic the Scottish bagpipes with a droning accompaniment, but there are some tricky fingerings to watch out for. In measures 7 and 15, see if you can make the left hand stretch with your little finger on #1a and your ring finger on #9 so you can play #5 with your index finger and #4a with your middle finger.

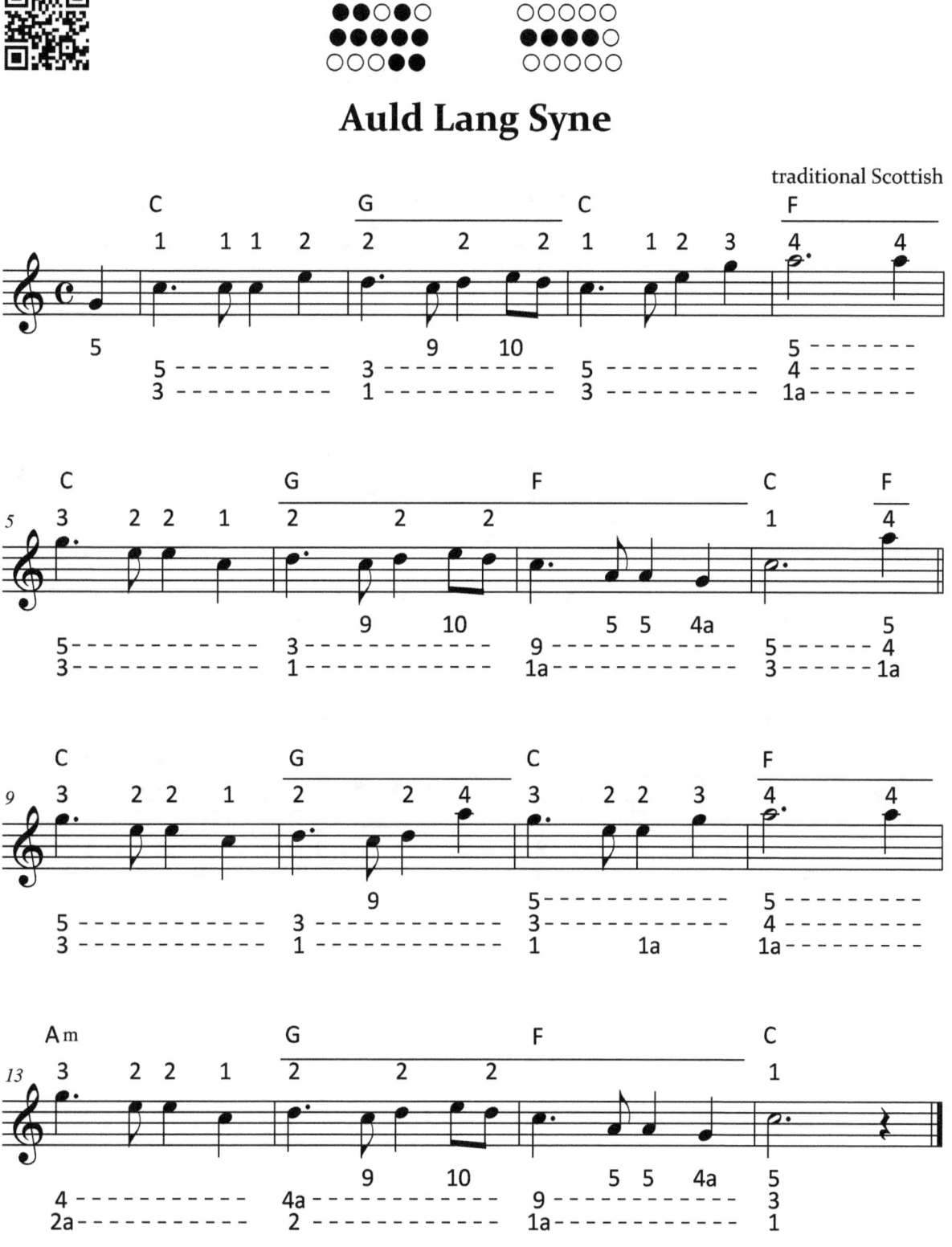

Auld Lang Syne

traditional Scottish

This tune is named for Harold Herrington, the first American maker of Anglo concertinas.

Buttons played

 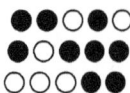  

Herrington Hall

Gary Coover

Copyright © 2010 Gary Coover, used by permission

Here's a good one to learn in the key of D minor, a lovely French waltz composed by Larry Wilson from East Texas.

Buttons played

You Are All I Have
(Vous êtes tout ce que j'ai)

Larry Wilson

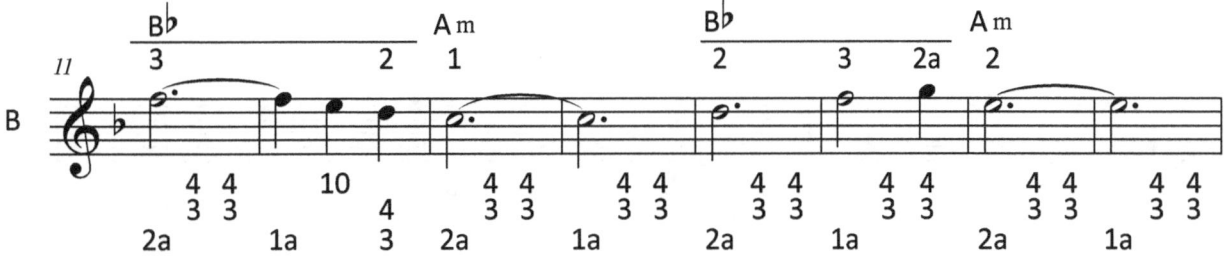

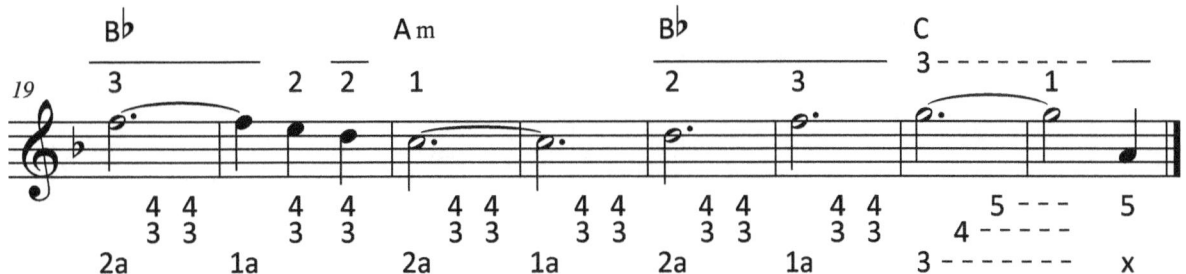

Arranged for concertina by Larry Wilson
Copyright © 2010 Larry Wilson, used by permission

This is a traditional processional Morris dance from the village of Winster in Derbyshire, England. It has been adopted by many Morris teams throughout the UK and USA as an excellent tune for a "Morris On".

Buttons played

  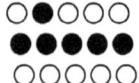 

Winster Processional

traditional English, as played by John Watcham

From the Ashley Hutchings CD "Son of Morris On"

Anglo Concertina in the Harmonic Style

"Leaping Jack" was the first tune written by concertina player John Kirkpatrick. This is a slightly simplified version to learn from, but try to snap the chords and make the tune leap.

Buttons played

Leaping Jack

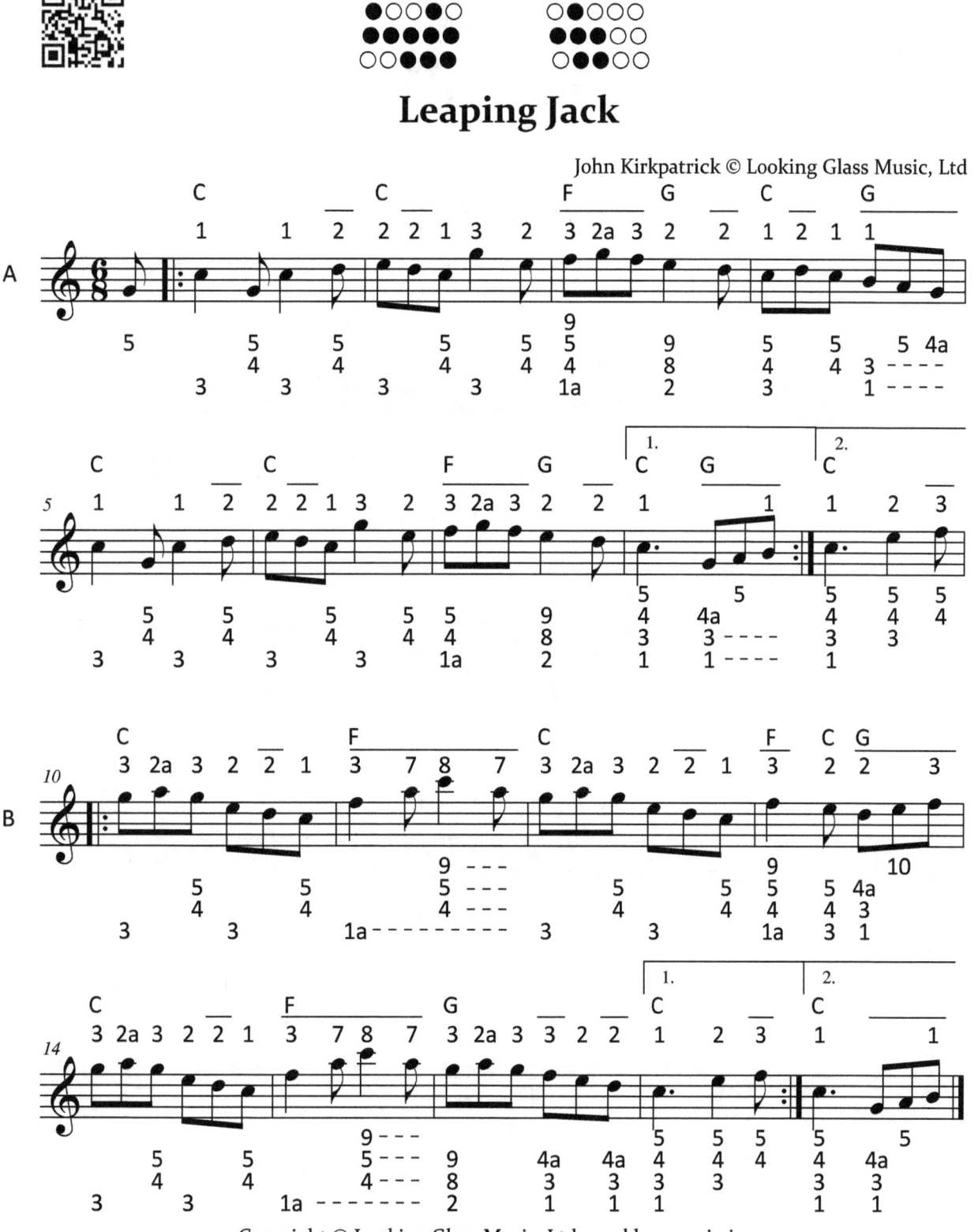

Copyright © Looking Glass Music, Ltd, used by permission
From the John Kirkpatrick CD "The Dance of the Demon Daffodils"

This traditional English morris tune from the village of Badby in Northamptonshire, England is also found in John Playford's "The English Dancing Master" from 1651. It is a great D minor tune with lots of opportunity for variations. Be sure to adjust your fingering in measure 11 to reach #10 with the index finger of your left hand while holding #2a & #4 steady.

Bobbing Joe

traditional English, as played by Andy Turner

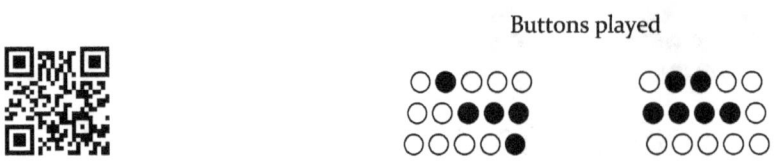

From the Magpie Lane CD "Speed the Plough"

Anglo Concertina in the Harmonic Style

This is a lovely waltz that was first published in Wales in 1802. Try to play this as lyrically as possible, imagine yourself in the beautiful Welsh countryside.

Buttons played

The Ash Grove
(AABA)

traditional Welsh

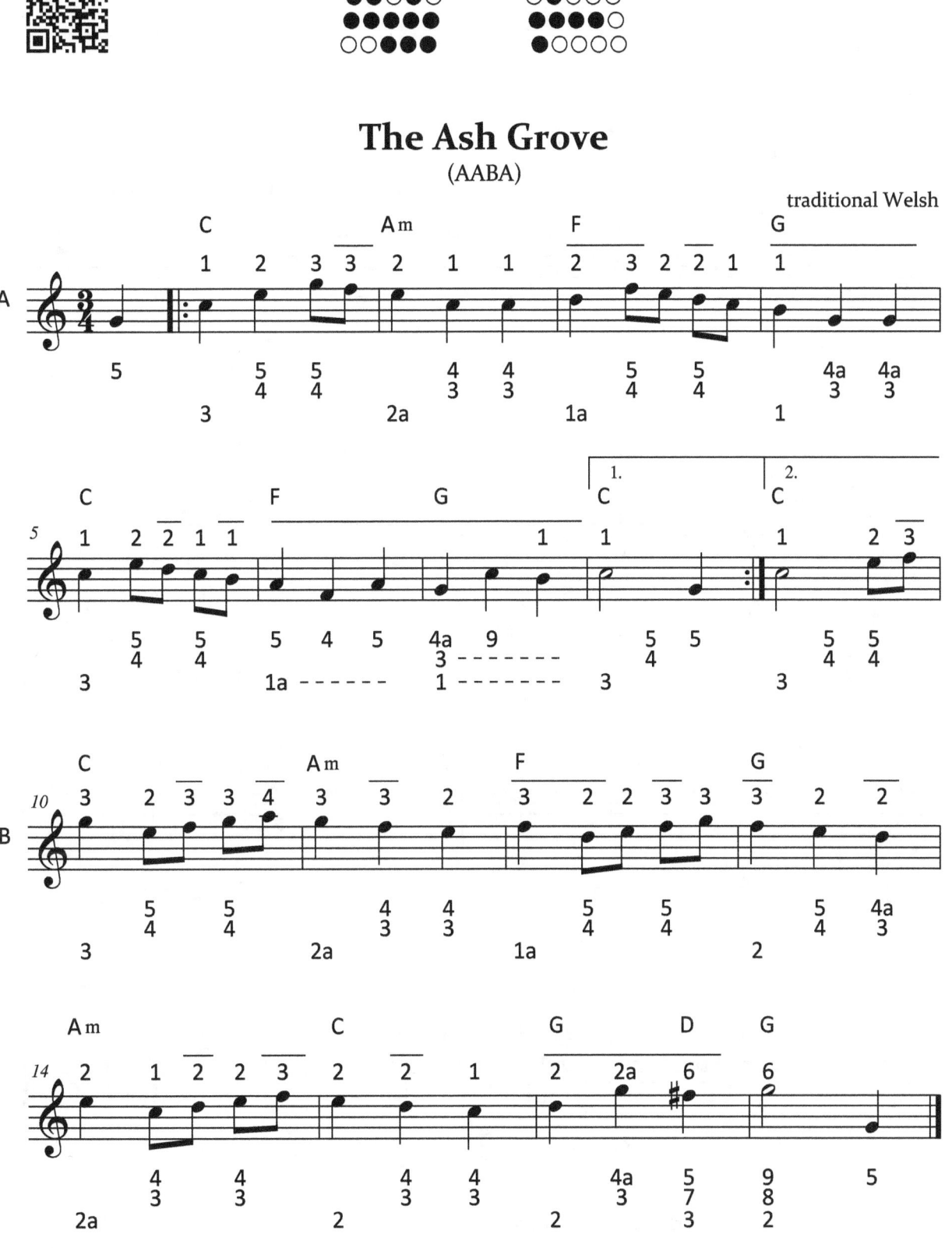

Here are two very different approaches to the same tune, first published in England by John Playford in 1651. Play this first version slow and stately.

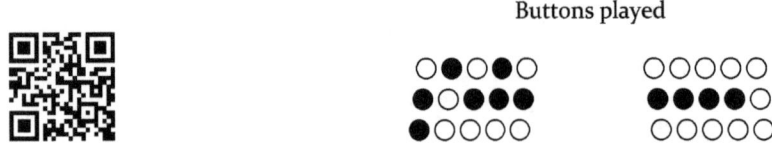

Parson's Farewell

traditional English, as played by Bertram Levy

From the Frank Ferrel & Bertram Levy LP "Sageflower Suite"

Now try this version which expresses the tune in a very different fashion. Play fairly fast and punch the chords hard.

Buttons played

Parson's Farewell

traditional English, as played by Adam Davis

This is a good tune for learning to play smoothly across different rows, and it has quite the classical pedigree. Composed in 1788 by Wolfgang Amadeus Mozart as part of his "Zwolf Deutsche Tanz", KV 536 No. 2 Trio, it appeared without a name in a tunebook owned by 19th century Sussex fiddler Michael Turner and has been known in the English folk world as Michael Turner's Waltz ever since.

Michael Turner's Waltz

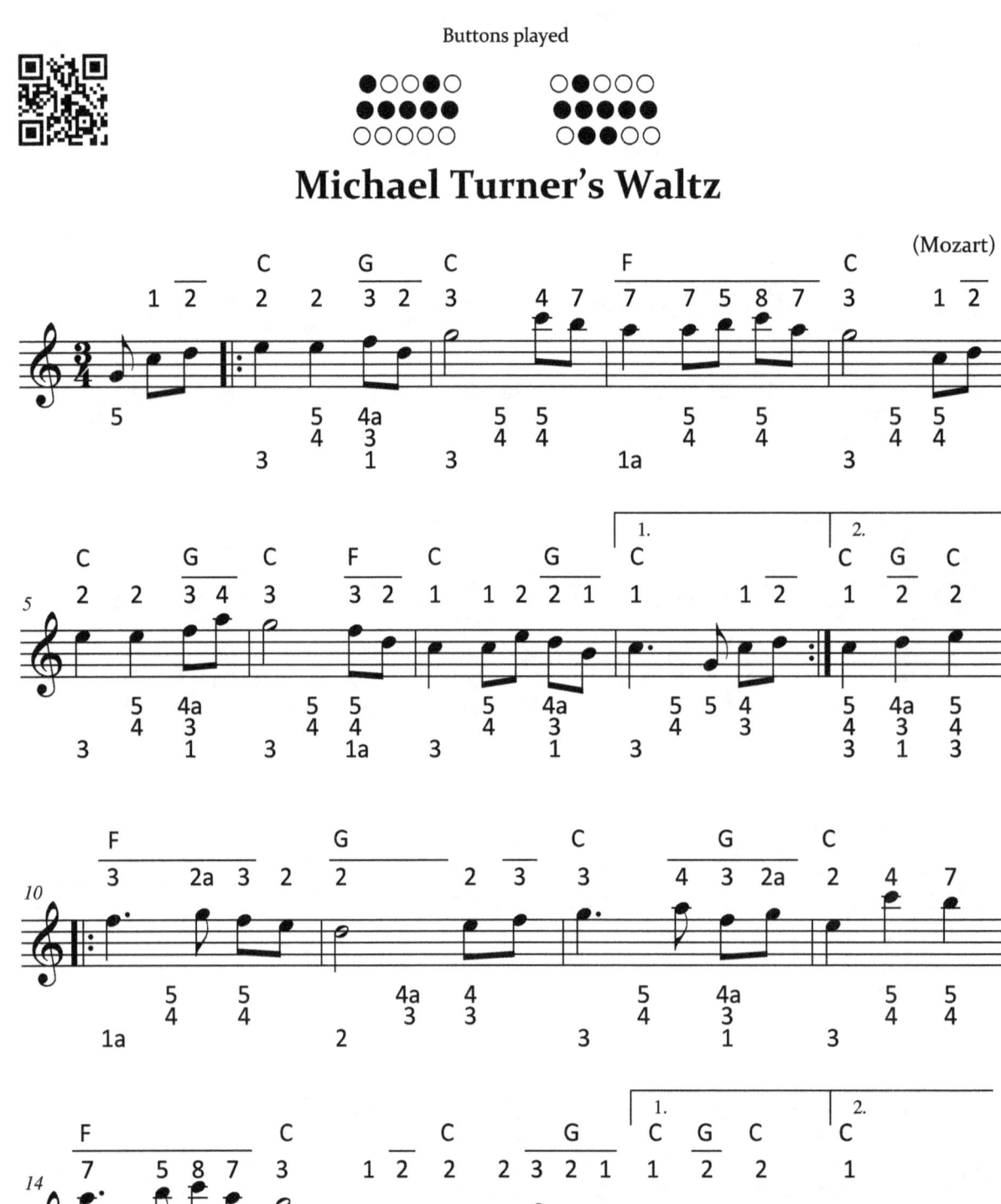

Anglo Concertina in the Harmonic Style

Chords are seldom set in stone, so let's try the same tune with a few subtle changes. For the 1985 Leicester Haymarket Theatre production of "Lark Rise", Ashley Hutchings and the Albion Band used "Michael Turner's Waltz" for the song *"Til the Time We Meet Again"*, adding some lovely new chords.

From the Lark Rise Band CD "Lark Rise Revisited"

Here's one everyone should know from primary and elementary school, as it's one of the most popular old English tunes, originating as a traditional Morris dance tune. Later in this tutor you'll find a very different version that was played by traditional concertina player William Kimber.

Buttons played

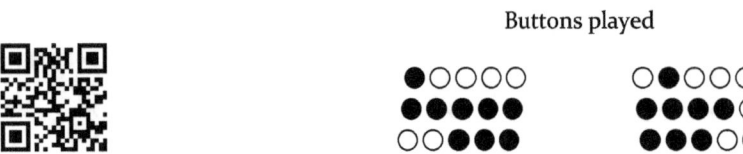

Country Gardens

traditional English

This is a beautiful Chinese love song learned from the singing of Liu Li Xin. Play it slowly and expressively.

Buttons played

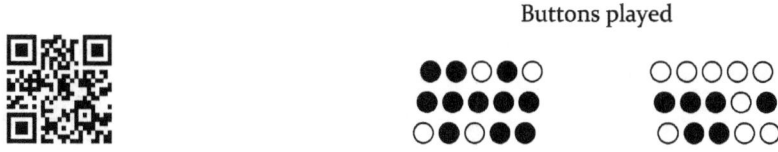

The Moon Knows My Heart
(AABA)

traditional Chinese

Anglo Concertina in the Harmonic Style

Another classic English Country Dance tune from the 1651 edition of "The English Dancing Master" by John Playford.

Buttons played

 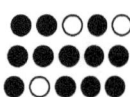  

Newcastle

traditional English

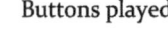

From the legendary Norfolk tradition of the Kipper Family from St Just-near-Trunch, this arrangement will give the little fingers on both hands a good workout.

Buttons played

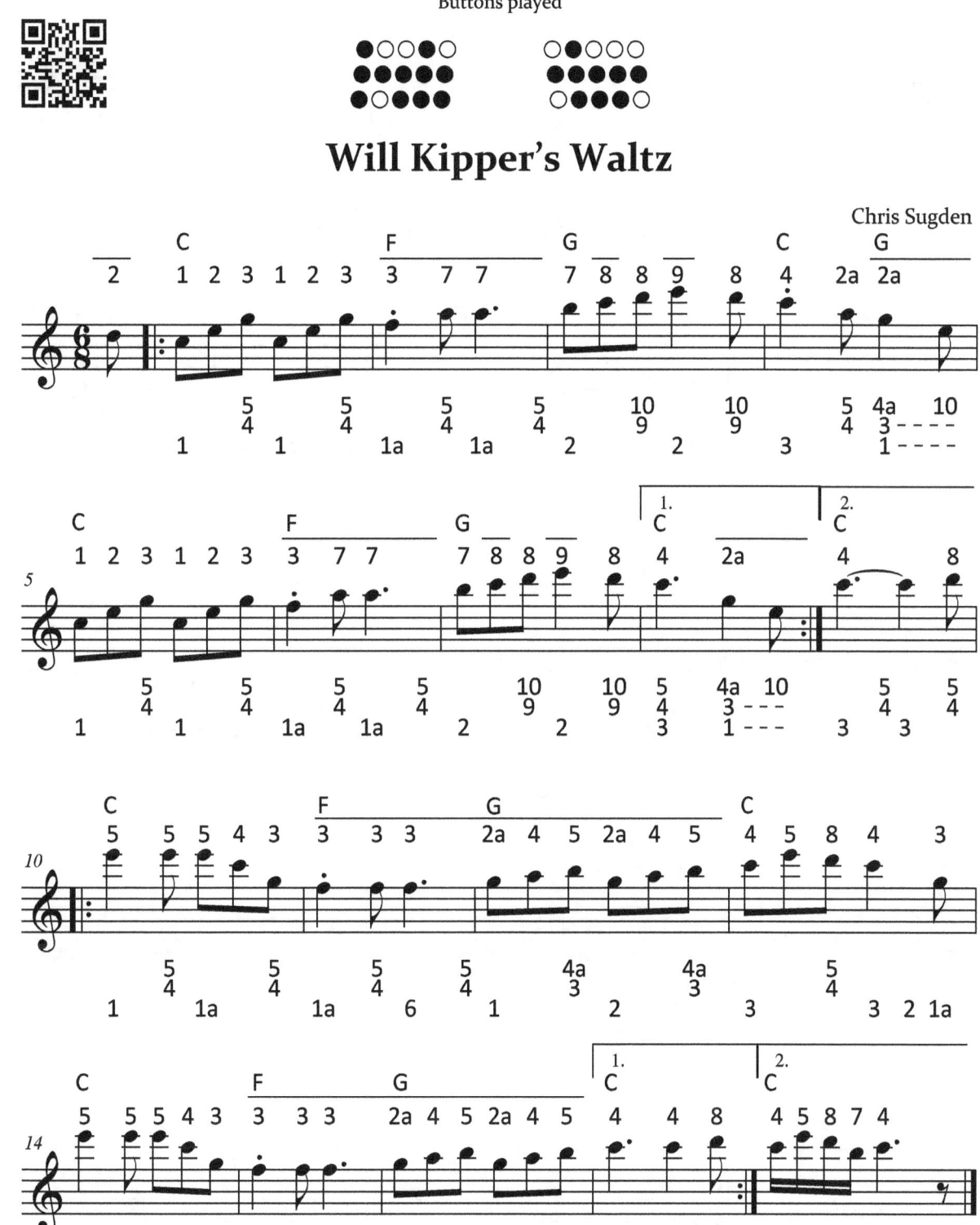

Copyright © 1986 Chris Sugden, used by permission

This is a slow Irish air learned from the beautiful singing of Cathy Jordan from the Irish band "Dervish". Since it is an air, do not follow the time signature rigidly but give it all the emotion you can to poetically express this unrequited love story.

Buttons played

For Ireland I'd Not Tell Her Name

traditional Irish

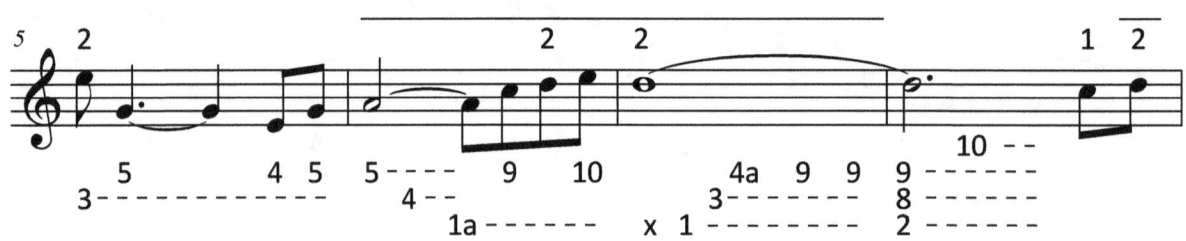

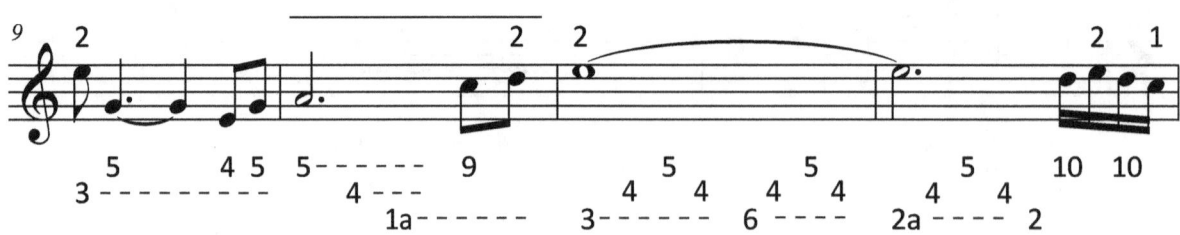

For Ireland I'd Not Tell Her Name (cont.)

From the Dervish CD "At the End of the Day"

Steve Hartz is an old-time musician from Nacogdoches, Texas, who has written many new tunes in the old traditional style. Originally written in the key of F, this hornpipe has been transposed here to the key of C. Play all three parts lively and jauntily.

Buttons played

The Old & Lost Hornpipe

Steve Hartz

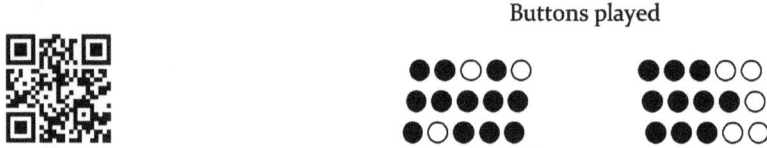

Old & Lost Hornpipe (cont.)

Copyright © 1998 Mystery Ridge Publishing B.M.I., used by permission

From the Steve Hartz CD "Crooked Steep & Rocky"

Here's a delightful English polka that was discovered in an old manuscript in Sheffield, England. Like a lot of polkas, the "A" part is in one key and the "B" part modulates to a key a fifth higher. Play this one briskly!

Buttons played

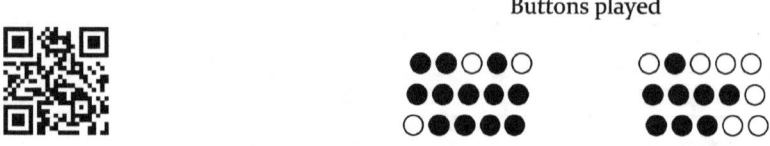

Fruits & Flowers

traditional English, as played by Keith Kendrick

From the Keith Kendrick CD "Home Ground"

First published about 1580, this tune has been popular for over 400 years. But it's not as simple to play on the Anglo as you might imagine. Here it is in Dm, which gives you a good workout on the third row in addition to some tricky fingering on the left side to smooth out the accompaniment.

Buttons played

Greensleeves

traditional English

Anglo Concertina in the Harmonic Style

This is a classic Irish song with words written in 1798 by Thomas Moore, but the tune is an ancient Irish melody (The Moreen) that possibly dates back to the 16th century. With a little creativity you can probably come up with variations that will use every button on the left hand side, and maybe even every button on the right hand side too.

Buttons played

The Minstrel Boy
(The Moreen)

traditional Irish

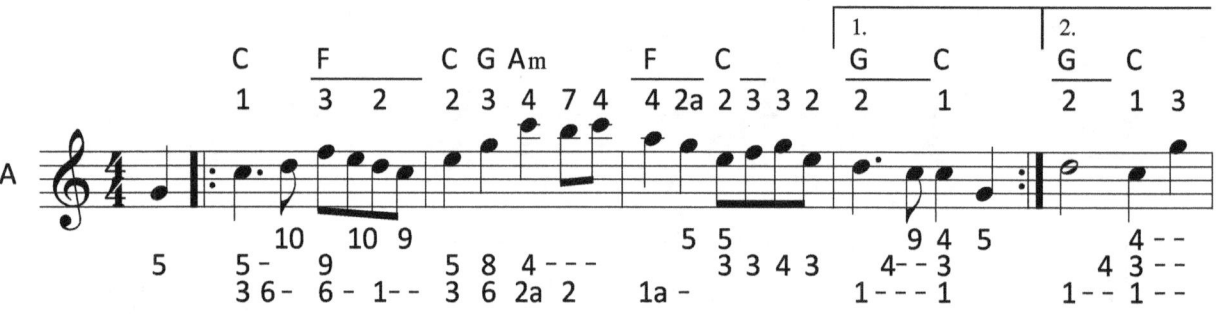

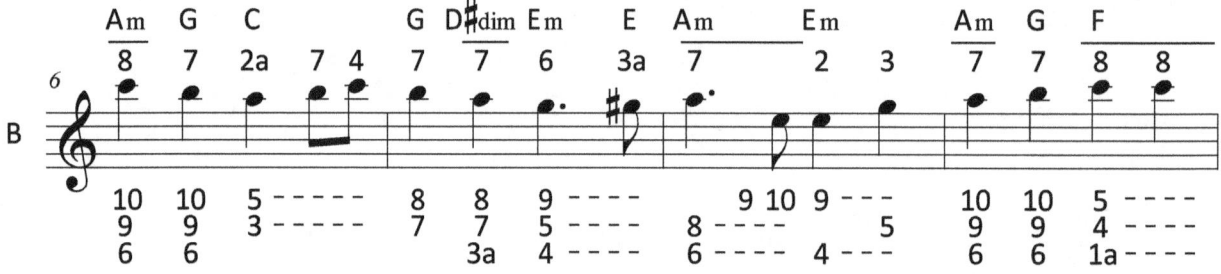

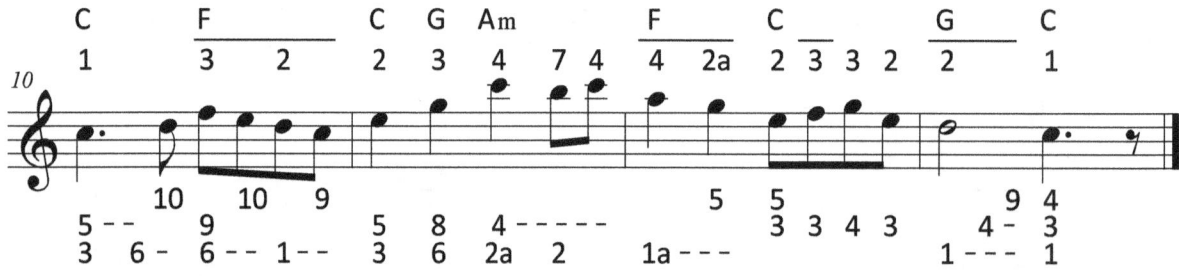

Anglo Concertina in the Harmonic Style

Ok, here's a real test for you – the same tune in four different keys! Composed by Michael Springer in 1976, it has often been mistakenly called "Bouchard's Hornpipe", "Broussard's Hornpipe", "Broushard's Hornpipe", etc. And through the years and vagaries of the "folk process" there are also many different variations of the tune being played. Here is the tune as originally written in the style of an old time fiddle tune.

Burchard's Hornpipe

Michael Springer

Copyright © 1976 Michael Springer, used by permission

This version was learned from the concertina playing of Jody Kruskal at a late night session at the Old Palestine Concertina Weekend in East Texas. Although usually played in the key of D, let's start off in the key of C:

Buttons played

Burchard's Hornpipe

Michael Springer

Copyright © 1976 Michael Springer, used by permission

Here it is in D, the key it was originally written in.

Buttons played

Burchard's Hornpipe

Michael Springer

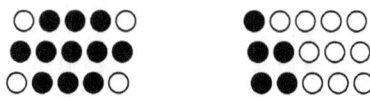

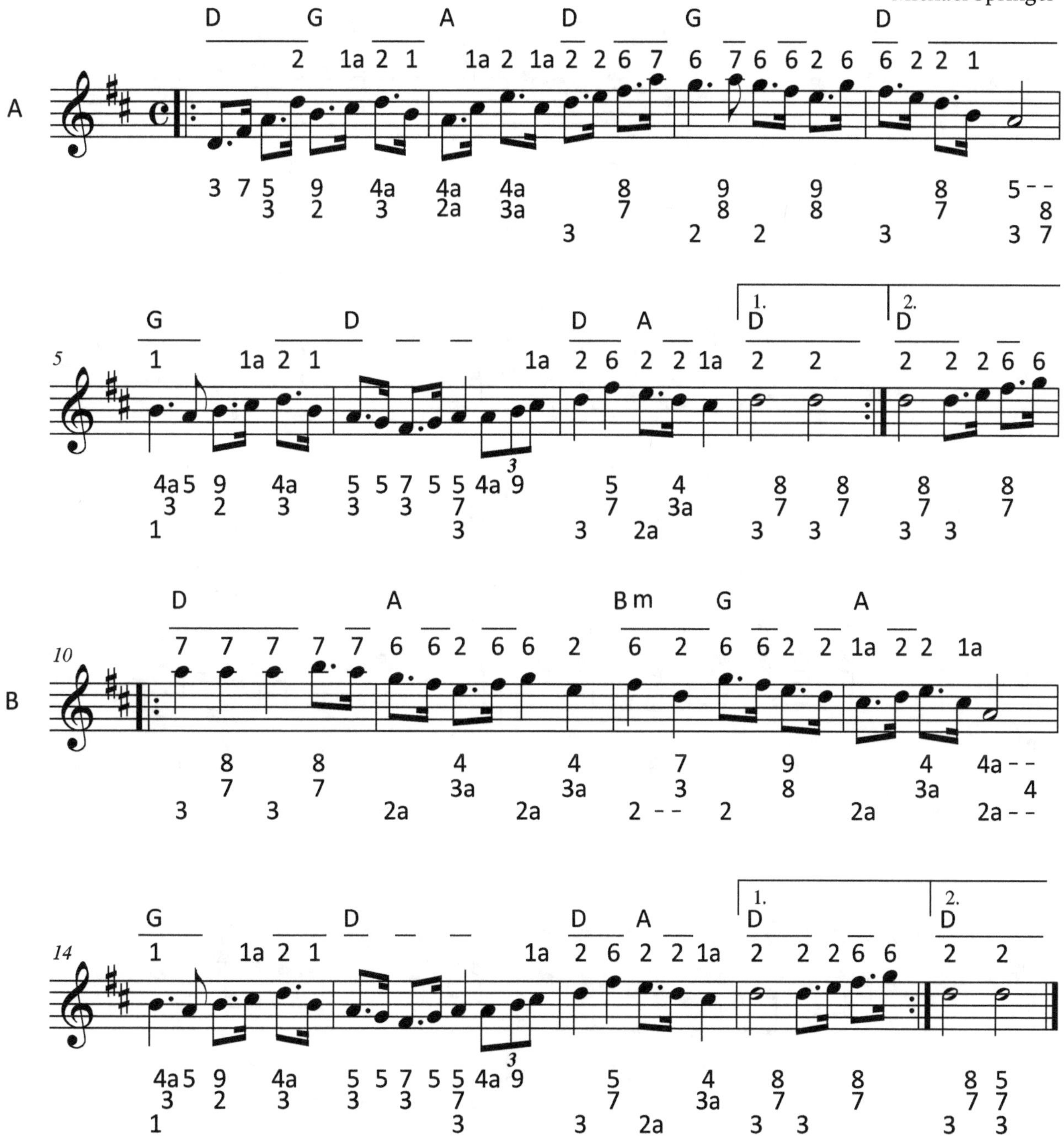

Copyright © 1976 Michael Springer, used by permission

It also works quite well in the key of G, and if you play this one on a G/D instrument, then you will be in the original key of D.

Buttons played

Burchard's Hornpipe

Michael Springer

Copyright © 1976 Michael Springer, used by permission

And just for fun, let's try it in the key of F:

Buttons played

Burchard's Hornpipe

Michael Springer

Copyright © 1976 Michael Springer, used by permission

We'll close out this section of the tutor with a jig composed by English fiddler John Dipper, son of famed concertina makers Colin & Rosalie Dipper. His tune has also undergone a little of the "folk process" - here is how he originally wrote it:

The Kennington Jig

John Dipper

Copyright © 2004 John Dipper, used by permission

And here it is transposed to the key of C and transcribed from the concertina playing of Jake Middleton. You gotta love those last three chords!

Buttons played

The Kennington Jig

John Dipper, as played by Jake Middleton

Copyright © 2004 John Dipper, used by permission

PERFORMER SHOWCASE

Now that you have a basic understanding of the Anglo concertina and know where most of the buttons are and when and how to use them, the following section presents note-for-note transcriptions of tunes recorded by well-known and world-renowned concertina players.

Although many of these performers play concertinas with more than 30-buttons, and sometimes with Jeffries accidentals on the right hand side, the tunes here have been painstakingly transcribed as closely as possible and adapted where necessary to fit on a standard 30-button Anglo with Wheatstone/Lachenal accidentals.

Short bios of each artist are included, as well as an extensive discography. These performers are the best in their field and you can learn a lot by studying their unique approaches to the concertina.

Not all of the listed recordings are currently in print, so it might take some resourcefulness on your part to track down all of them. It will be a quest well worth your effort. Listen to their recordings, study their playing styles and nuances, and with enough skill and practice you will eventually be able to play along.

Some of these musicians also have tune books and tutors, and additional recordings and videos can often be found online at www.youtube.com and other internet sites.

Many of these concertina players can be seen and heard at festivals and workshops, or perhaps even in the street outside a pub accompanying a Morris Dance team. Find them, learn from them, support them, and enjoy their playing!

William Kimber (1872-1961)

Known as the Father of English Morris Dancing, William Kimber was a direct link to the tradition and was the first Anglo concertina player ever recorded. His historical style is unique among Anglo players, and his playing style was learned directly from his father and forefathers.

Perhaps the most famous tune learned from Kimber is "Country Gardens", a traditional Morris dance from Headington Quarry in Oxfordshire, England.

For more information on Kimber's music and playing style, see the combination tune book and history book "The Anglo Concertina Music of William Kimber" by Dan M. Worrall (EFDSS 2005).

Recommended Recordings:
William Kimber – *The Art of William Kimber* – Topic (1974) 12T249
William Kimber – *Absolutely Classic, the Music of William Kimber* – EFDSS (1999) CD03

Buttons played

Country Gardens

traditional English, as played by William Kimber

Transcribed by Dan Worrall from a 1948 recording released later on EFDSS CD03, used by permission

Anglo Concertina in the Harmonic Style

John Kirkpatrick

Perhaps the best known Anglo concertina player today, John has a boisterous, fully chorded style that is especially suitable for English Country, Morris and Border dancing, yet he is also a master of subtle and effective song accompaniment.

John has performed as a solo artist on concertina, melodeon and button accordion since the early 1960's, and has been a member of the Albion Country Band, Band of Hope, Brass Monkey, The Richard Thompson Band, Steeleye Span, and Umps & Dumps. He also founded the Shropshire Bedlams, a Border dance troupe known for their unique antics and dancing style.

Recommended Recordings:
John Kirkpatrick – *Jump At The Sun* – Leader (1972) LER2033
Ashley Hutchings – *Morris On* – Island (1972) HELP5
Hutchings & Kirkpatrick – *Compleat Dancing Master* – Island (1974) HELP17
John Kirkpatrick & Sue Harris – *The Rose of Britain's Isle* – Topic (1974) 12TS247
Albion Country Band – *Battle of the Field* – Island (1976) HELP25
Kirkpatrick & Harris – *Among the Many Attractions* – Topic (1976) 12TS295
John Kirkpatrick – *Plain Capers* – Free Reed/Topic (1976/1992) TSCD458
John Kirkpatrick & Sue Harris – *Shreds & Patches* – Topic (1977) 12TS355
John Kirkpatrick – *Going Spare* – Free Reed (1978) FRR0030
John Kirkpatrick & Sue Harris – *Facing the Music* – Topic (1980) 12TS408
John Kirkpatrick – *Sheepskins* – Squeezer (1988) SQZ125
John Kirkpatrick – *Earthling* – MW Records (1994) MWCD4006
The John Kirkpatrick Band – *Force of Habit* – Fledg'ling (1996) FLED3007
The John Kirkpatrick Band – *Welcome to Hell* – Fledg'ling (1997) FLED3011
John Kirkpatrick – *One Man & His Box* – MW Records (1998) MWCD4024
John Kirkpatrick – *Orlando's Return* – Mally (2003) DMPC0301
John Kirkpatrick – *Garrick's Delight* – Mally (2003) DMPCD0302
John Kirkpatrick – *The Duck Race* – Fledg'ling (2004) FLED3043
Various – *Anglo International* – FolkSound (2005) FSCD70
John Kirkpatrick – *Make No Bones* – Fledg'ling (2007) FLED3065
John Kirkpatrick – *The Dance of the Demon Daffodils* – Fledg'ling (2009) FLED3075
John Kirkpatrick – *God Speed the Plough* – Fledg'ling (2011) FLED3084
John Kirkpatrick – *Every Mortal Place* – Fledg'ling (2012) FLED3089

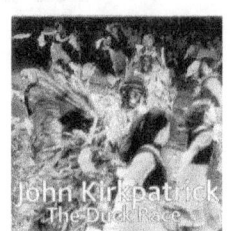

Tunebooks: "Opus Pocus" – DragonflyMusic (1988)
"Jump at the Sun" – Quarry Publishing (2010)

Tunes:
1. Fair Play
2. King George III's Minuet
3. The Charabanc Schottische
4. Hanged I Shall Be
5. Petal of Spice

Website: www.johnkirkpatrick.co.uk

Fair Play

Buttons played

Sally Kirkpatrick © Squeezer Music
as played by John Kirkpatrick

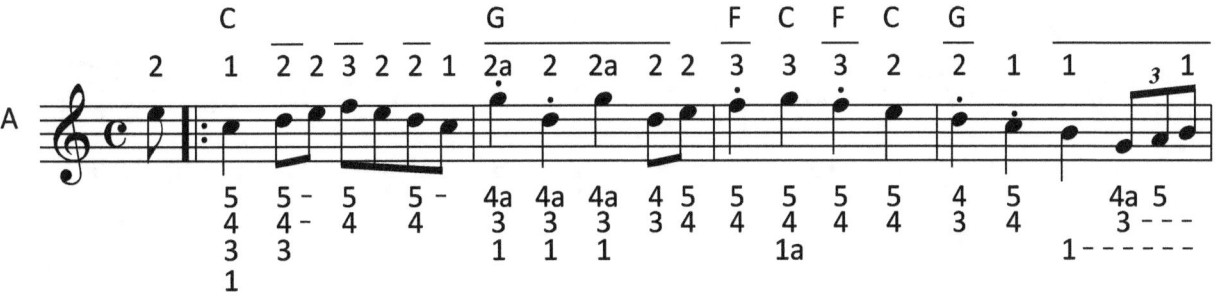
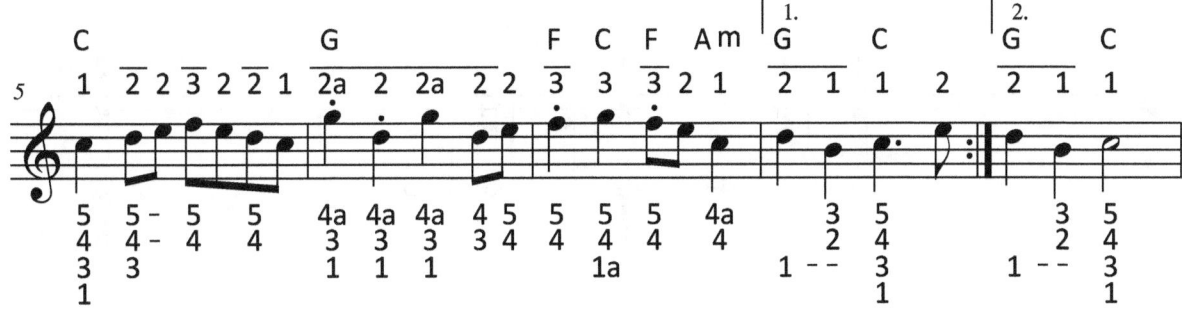
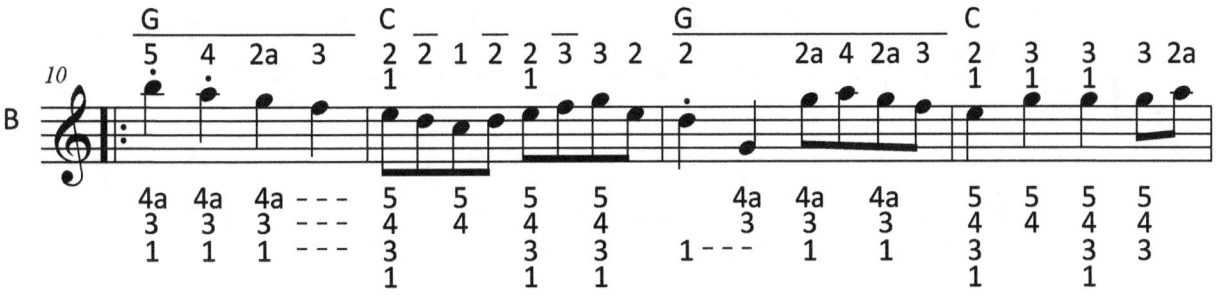

Copyright © Squeezer Music, used by permission
From the John Kirkpatrick CD "The Duck Race"

Anglo Concertina in the Harmonic Style

King George III's Minuet

Buttons played

c. 1794, as played by John Kirkpatrick

From the John Kirkpatrick CD "Make No Bones"

The Charabanc Schottische

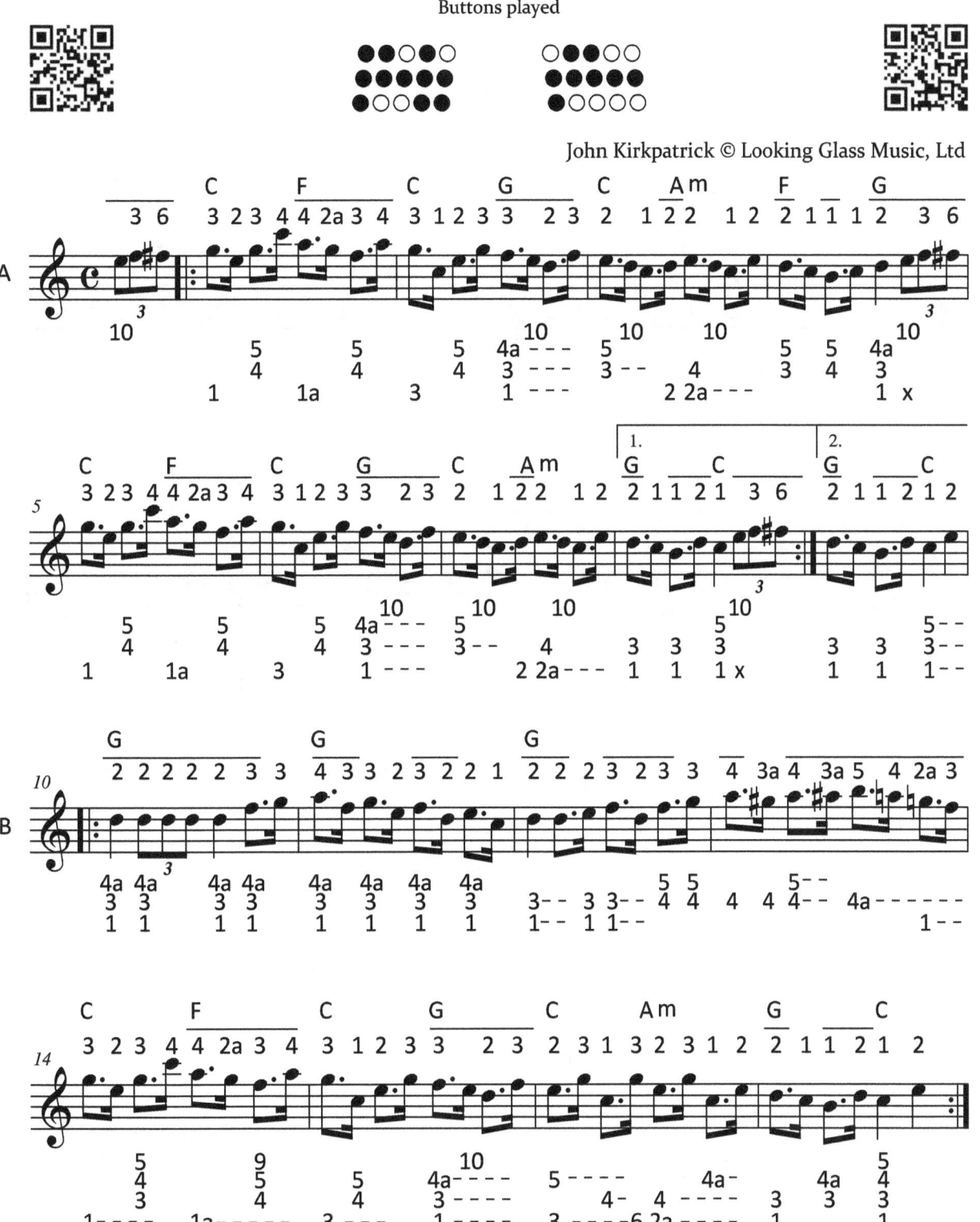

Hanged I Shall Be

Buttons played

traditional English, as played by John Kirkpatrick

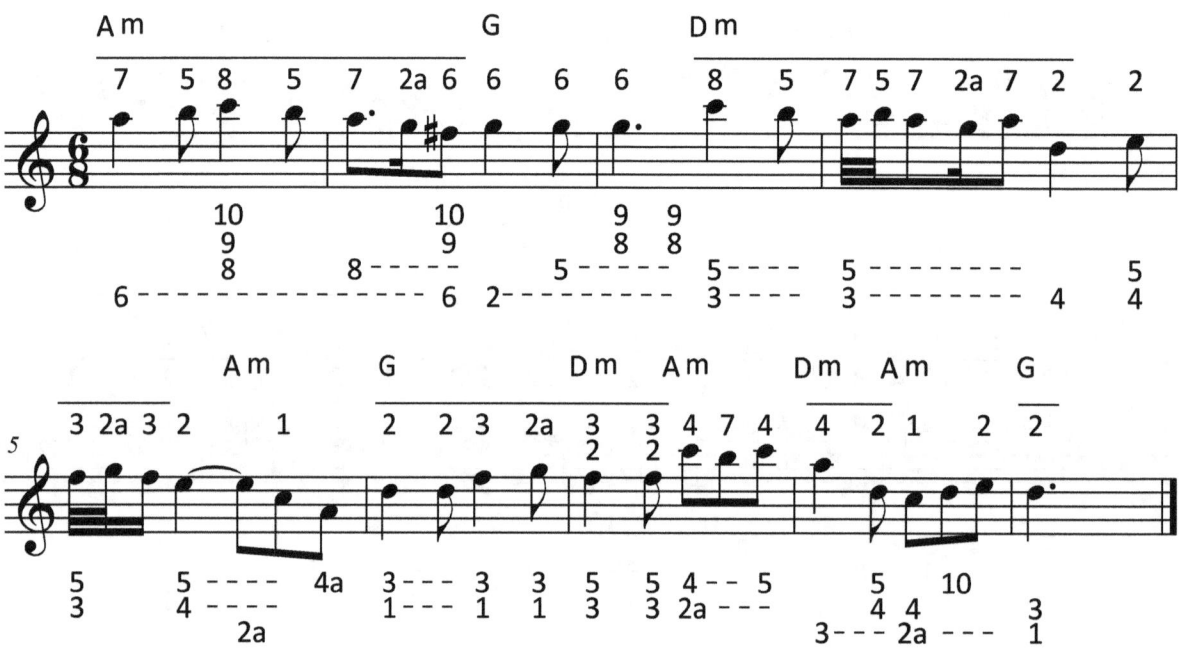

From the Albion Country Band CD "Battle of the Field"

Petal of Spice

Buttons played

  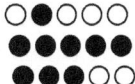 

John Kirkpatrick © Squeezer Music

Copyright © Squeezer Music, used by permission
From the John Kirkpatrick CD "The Dance of the Demon Daffodils"

Anglo Concertina in the Harmonic Style

Jody Kruskal

An enthusiastic performer, teacher, composer, singer and dance caller, Jody specializes in writing new tunes for the concertina as well as playing traditional American Old-Time songs and dance music. He plays the Anglo concertina in a very full and energetic style that at times is reminiscent of an old time fully chorded harmonica.

He sometimes performs with "Henry", a planchet marionette puppet controlled by a single string attached to his knee. While singing and accompanying with the concertina, Jody bounces his leg and Henry dances to the music.

Although Jody mostly plays an Anglo concertina in the key of G/D, he can also play C/G and taught the following two tunes in his "Old Time Music for Anglo" workshop at the Old Palestine Concertina Weekend in East Texas in 2011.

Recommend Recordings
Grand Picnic – *Grand Picnic* – Dean Street Music (2002) DSM103
Various – *Anglo International* – FolkSound (2005) FSCD70
Jody Kruskal – *Naked Concertina* – Kruskal (2006)
Jody Kruskal – *Poor Little Liza Jane* – Kruskal (2006)
Jody Kruskal & Paul Friedman – *Paul & Jody* – Kruskal (2009) JKM104
Jody Kruskal – *Sing to Me Concertina Boy* – Kruskal (2012)

Tunebooks
"Feet in the Clouds" – Jody Kruskal
"Cool Tunes for Hot Dances" – Jody Kruskal

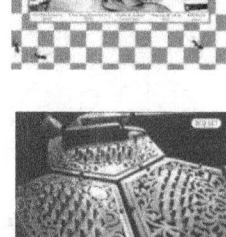

Tunes

1. Fly Around My Pretty Little Miss
2. Elk River Blues

Website: www.jodykruskal.com

Fly Around My Pretty Little Miss

Buttons played

traditional American, as played by Jody Kruskal

From Jody Kruskal's workshop "Old Time Music for Anglo Concertina" at Palestine, Texas, 2011
Concertina arrangement copyright © Jody Kruskal, used by permission

Elk River Blues

Bertram Levy

A legendary American concertina performer, Bertram is also the author of two concertina tutors: "The Anglo Concertina De-Mystified" (1985) and "American Fiddle Styles for the Anglo Concertina" (2011).

His album 1978 "Sageflower Suite" with Frank Ferrel is considered by many to be one of the finest examples of concertina and fiddle music accompanying each other, with amazing dynamics and interplay between the two instruments. In 2012 he recorded an album of old-time concertina and fiddle music with Kirk Sutphin.

Bertram is a highly sought-after concertina performer and teacher. He also plays the bandoneon, a much more complex Argentinian cousin of the Anglo concertina, and is leader of the band "Tangoheart". A self-proclaimed bandoneonista, moved to Buenos Aires in 2005 to study at the Conservatorio de Manuel de Falla with Rodolfo Daluisio.

Recommend Recordings
Frank Ferrel & Bertram Levy – *Sageflower Suite* – Sageflower (1978) LF001
Bertram Levy & Peter Ostroushko – *First Generation* – Flying Fish (1986) FF392
Various – *Anglo International* – FolkSound (2005) FSCD70
Bertram Levy & Kirk Sutphin – *The Bellow and the Bow* – Bertram Levy Music Productions (2012) BLMP4

Books
"The Anglo Concertina Demystified" – Bertram Levy (1985)
"American Fiddle Styles for the Anglo Concertina" – Bertram Levy (2011)

Tunes
1. Bride's March
2. The New Rigged Ship

Website: www.bertramlevy.com

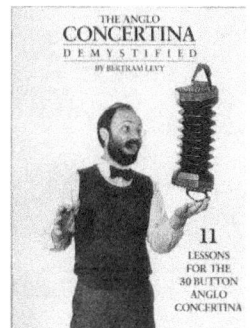

Anglo Concertina in the Harmonic Style

Bride's March

Buttons played

traditional Swedish, as played by Bertram Levy

From the Frank Ferrel & Bertram Levy LP "Sageflower Suite"
Concertina arrangement by Bertram Levy, used by permission

The New Rigged Ship

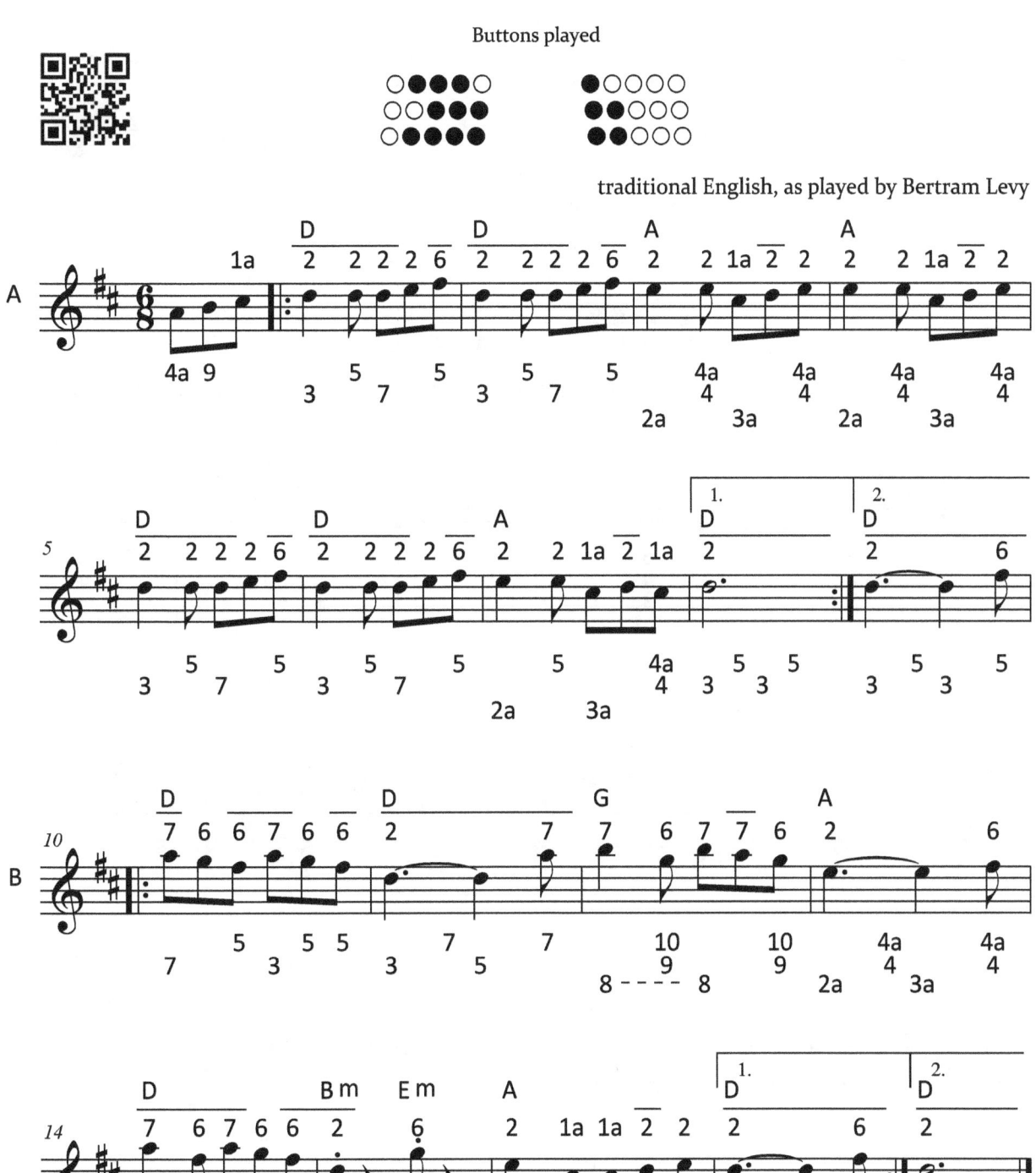

traditional English, as played by Bertram Levy

From the Bertram Levy book & CD "The Anglo Concertina Demystified"
Concertina arrangement by Bertram Levy, used by permission

Reverend Kenneth N.J. Loveless (1911-1995)

"Father Kenneth" was a well-loved local vicar and musician who learned how to play the concertina directly from William Kimber. A fixture on the English folk scene for many years, he often played an Anglo concertina originally given to Kimber in 1909 (seen here in photo taken in 1979).

The Nutting Girl

Buttons played

traditional English, as played by Father Kenneth Loveless

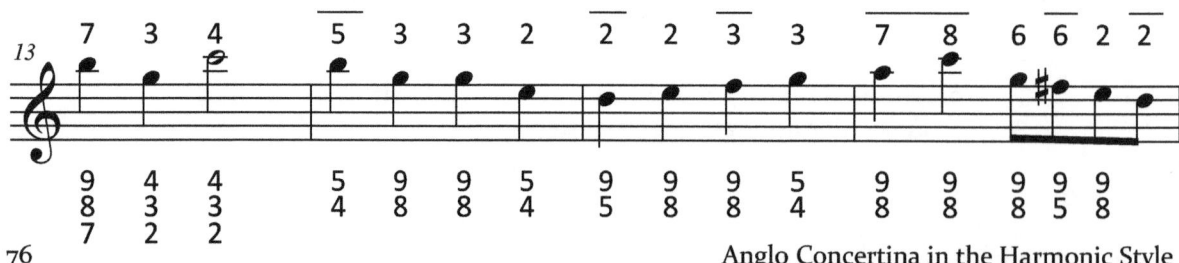

Anglo Concertina in the Harmonic Style

The Nutting Girl (cont.)

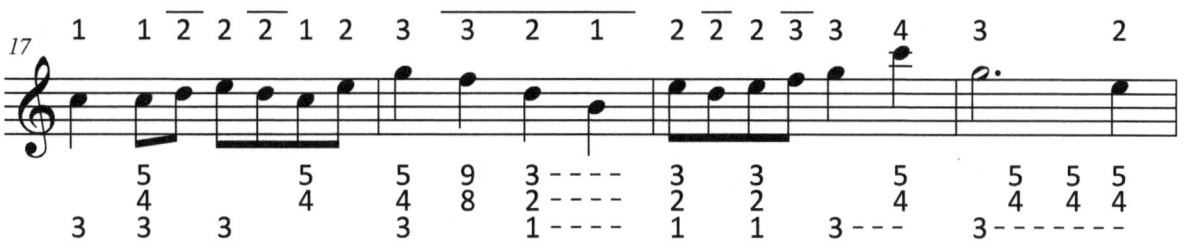

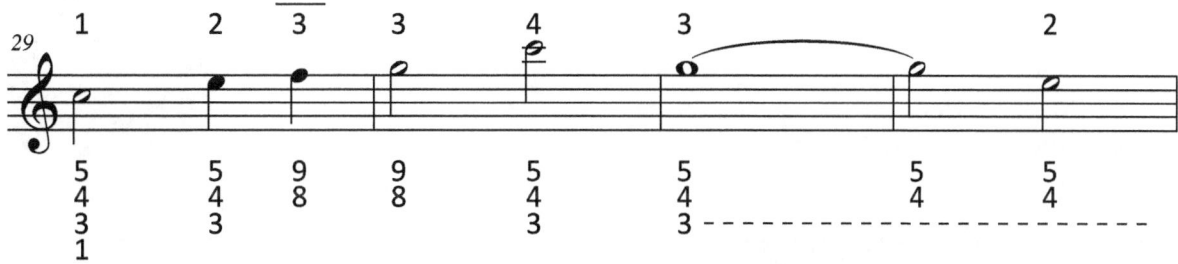

From the CD "The Magic of Morris"

Brian Peters

A multi-instrumentalist who sings, plays guitar, melodeon and Anglo concertina, Brian has developed an incredibly varied style of concertina playing, including everything from dance tunes to laments to classical music to pop standards.

Brian is well established in the English folk music world as a singer of traditional ballads and songs, and in addition to being a top melodeon player is also a popular teacher and performer on the Anglo concertina. He has played major folk festivals in Britain, Australia, New Zealand, the USA and Canada, and has toured extensively in Europe.

Recommended Recordings
Brian Peters – *Persistence of Memory* – Fellside (1985) FE051
Brian Peters – *Fools of Fortune* – Harbourtown (1989) HAR005
Brian Peters – *Seeds of Time* – Harbourtown (1992) HAR021
Brian Peters – *Squeezing Out Sparks* – Pugwash Records (1994) PUG001
Brian Peters & Gordon Tyrall – *Clear the Road* – Harbourtown (1996) HAR031
Brian Peters – *Sharper Than The Thorn* – Pugwash Records (1997) PUG002
Brian Peters – *The Beast in the Box* – Pugwash Records (1998) PUG003
Brian Peters & Gordon Tyrall – *The Moving Moon* – Gaho Music (2000) GAH03
Brian Peters – *Lines* – Pugwash Records (2001) PUG004
Brian Peters – *Different Tongues* – Pugwash Records (2003) PUG005
Brian Peters – *Anglophilia* – Pugwash Records (2005) PUG006
Brian Peters – *Songs of Trial and Triumph* – Pugwash Records (2008) PUG007
Brian Peters – *Gritstone Serenade* – Pugwash Records (2010) PUG008

Tunes
1. Nymph
2. Sweet Sorrow
3. Adieu My Lovely Nancy
4. Accordion Tune

Tunebook
"Rattle and Roll" – Brian Peters

Website: www.harbourtownrecords.com/peters.html

Nymph

Buttons played

traditional English, as played by Brian Peters

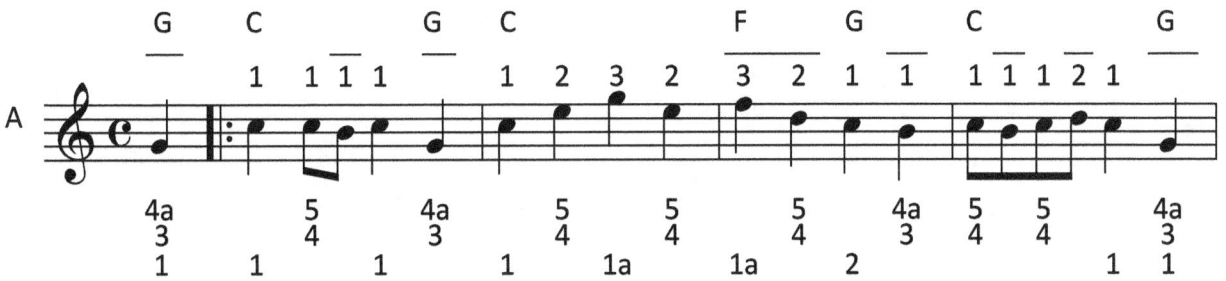

From the Brian Peters CD "Anglophilia"

Sweet Sorrow

Buttons played

 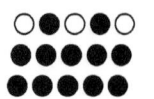  

Brian Peters

Copyright © Brian Peters, used by permission
From the Brian Peters CD "Anglophilia"

Adieu My Lovely Nancy

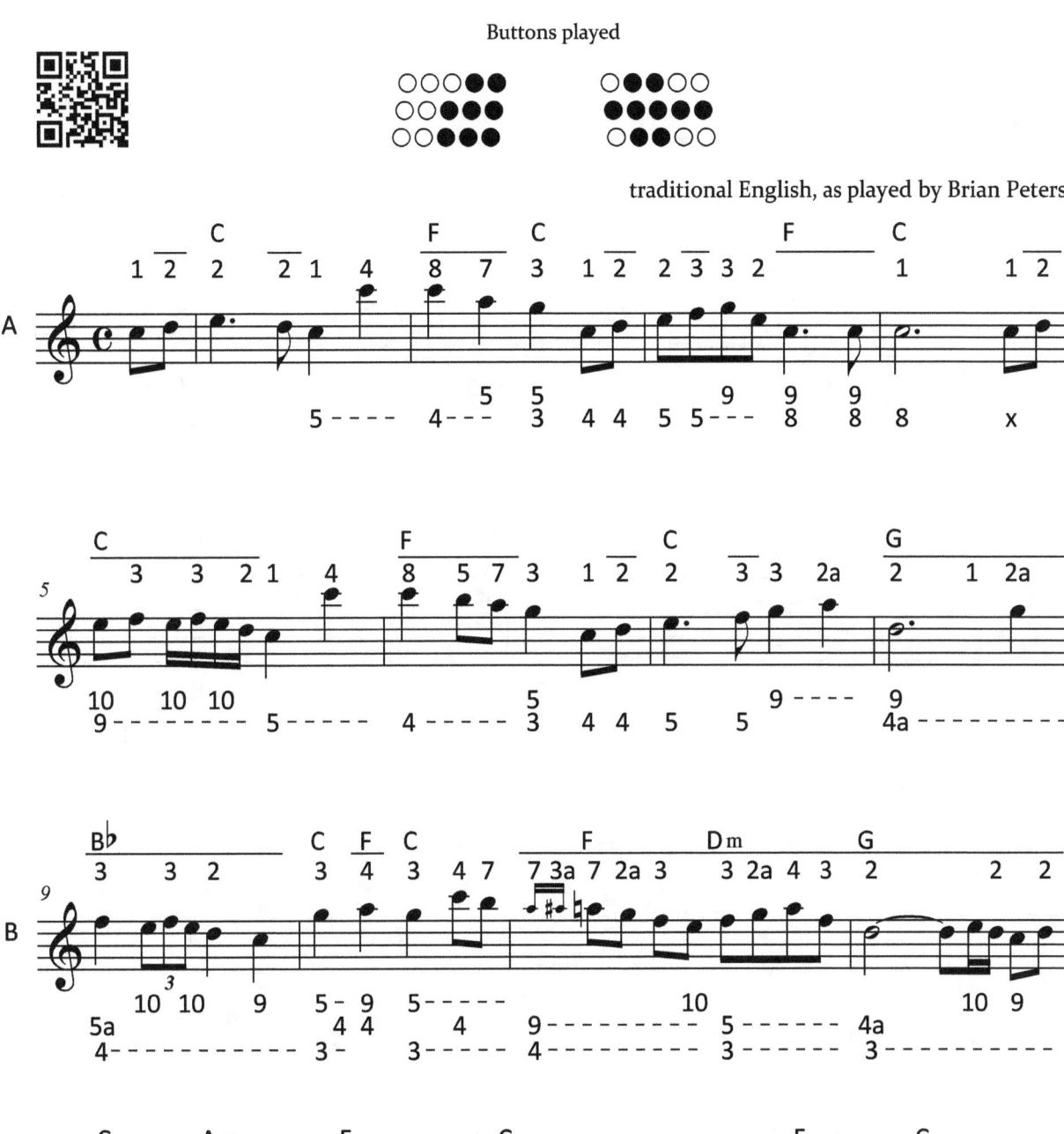

traditional English, as played by Brian Peters

From the Brian Peters CD "Anglophilia"

Accordion Tune

Andy Turner

Perhaps best known for his playing and singing with the English folk group Magpie Lane, Andy plays the Anglo concertina in a very precise and graceful style with very simple yet highly effective harmonic accompaniment. Instead of handfuls of chords in the left hand, he often creates beautiful harmonies with only single or double notes on the left hand side.

Andy has played and danced for Oyster Morris and was briefly a member of the Oyster Band. He played in a duo with Chris Wood before joining Magpie Lane, and now plays with fiddler Mat Green and is a member of the electric folk band Geckoes.

Recommended Recordings

Andy Turner – *Love, Death and The Cossack* – Audinary (1990) AUD001
Geckoes – *Geckoblaster* – Ock Records (1992) OCK002
Magpie Lane – *The Oxford Ramble* – Beautiful Jo (1993) BEJOCD3
Magpie Lane – *Speed the Plough* – Beautiful Jo (1994) BEJOCD 4
Magpie Lane – *Wassail* – Beautiful Jo (1995) BEJOCD 8
Geckoes – *Art Gecko* – Ock Records (1995) OCK003GTi
Magpie Lane – *Jack in the Green* – Beautiful Jo (1998) BEJOCD22
Geckoes – *The Red Horse* – Ock Records (1999) OCK060
Magpie Lane – *A Taste of Ale* – Beautiful Jo (2000) BEJOCD32
Magpie Lane – *Six for Gold* – Beautiful Jo (2002) BEJOCD 42
Various – *Anglo International* – FolkSound (2005) FSCD70
Magpie Lane – *Knock at the Knocker, Ring at the Bell* – Beautiful Jo (2006) BEJOCD 52
Magpie Lane – *The Robber Bird* – Magpie Lane (2011) MLCD008

Tunes

1. Swaggering Boney
2. Packington's Pound
3. Old Molly Oxford
4. Eastwell Park

Website: www.magpielane.co.uk/andyturner

Swaggering Boney
(Longborough)

Buttons played

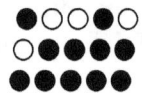

traditional English, as played by Andy Turner

[Musical notation with tablature]

From the Magpie Lane CD "Speed the Plough"

Packington's Pound

Old Molly Oxford
(Fieldtown)

Buttons played

 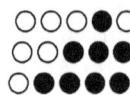 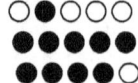

traditional English, as played by Andy Turner

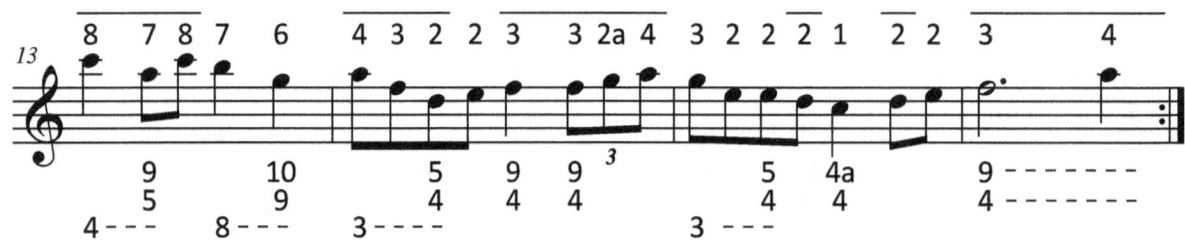

From the Magpie Lane CD "The Oxford Ramble"

Eastwell Park

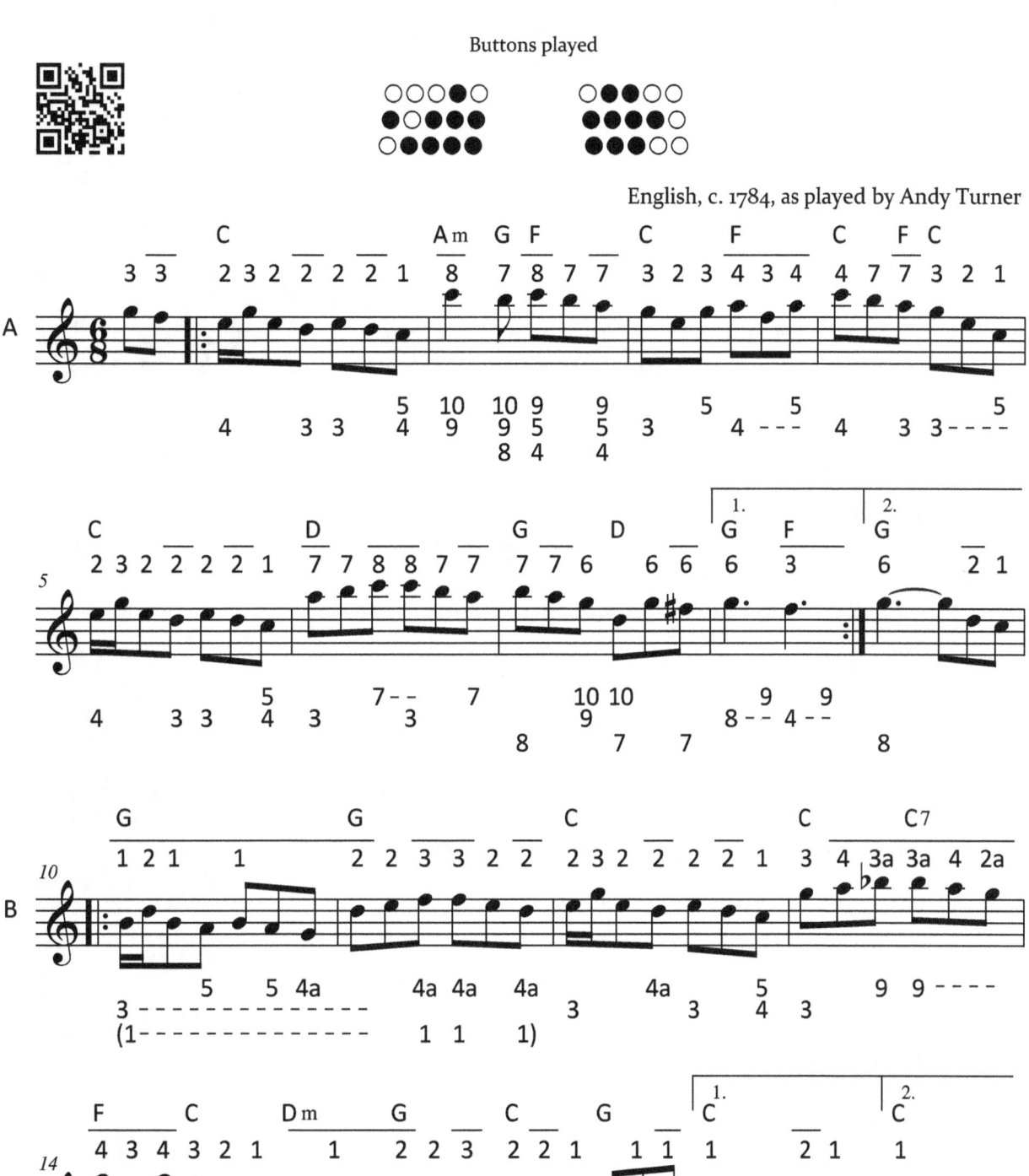

From the CD "Anglo International"

John Watcham

Although his recordings are few and far between, John's contribution to Anglo concertina playing is immense. Specializing in traditional Morris dance music for many years, he has developed a solid dance style that often incorporates a unique and very active walking bass line.

John started out as the musician for the Chingford Morris Men, and later played for the Albion Morris Men. He has recorded with Shirley Collins, and with the folkrock Albion Band on the "Son of Morris On" album. He was also the uncredited concertina player on the Ashley Hutchings' "Rattlebone & Ploughjack" album. John performed with Michael Clifton in the Victorian duo known as "Mr Gladstone's Bag", and is currently the concertina player for Brighton Morris.

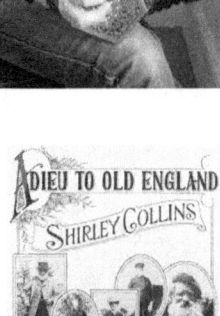

Recommended Recordings:
Shirley Collins – *Adieu to Old England* (1974) – Topic 12TS238
BBC Four TV – *Electric Folk* (1974)
Ashley Hutchings – *Son of Morris On* (1976/2003) – EMI SHSM2012 / Talking Elephant TECD038
Ashley Hutchings – *Rattlebone & Ploughjack* (1976/1997) – Island/BGO BGOCD353
Shirley Collins – *Amaranth* (1976) – EMI SHSM2008
Buz Collins – *Water and Rain* (1998) – Fellside FECD139
Albion Morris – *Still Dancing After All These Years* (2002) – AlbionMorris FOAD 30/CD
Various – *Anglo International* (2005) – FolkSound FSCD70

Tunes
1. Monck's March
2. Black Joker
3. Cuckoo's Nest
4. Lumps of Plum Pudding
5. Fieldtown Processional

Monck's March
(Bledington)

Buttons played

 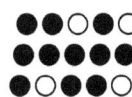  

traditional English, as played by John Watcham

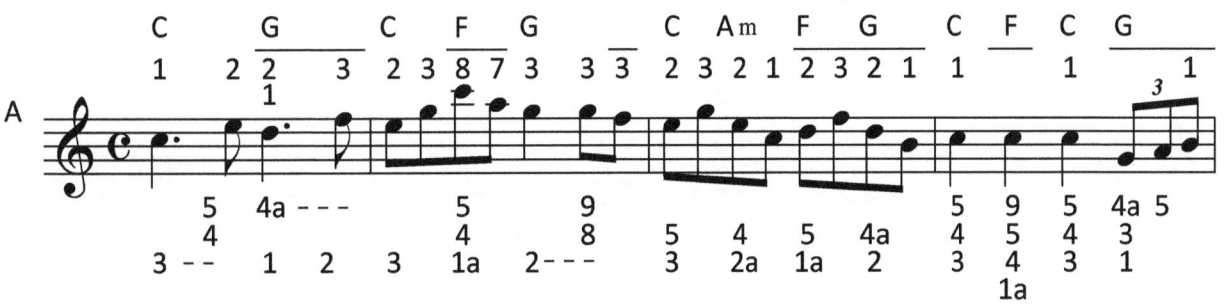
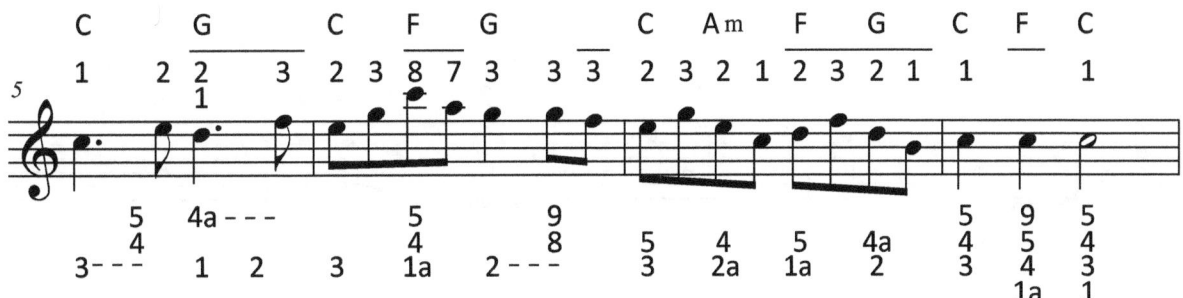

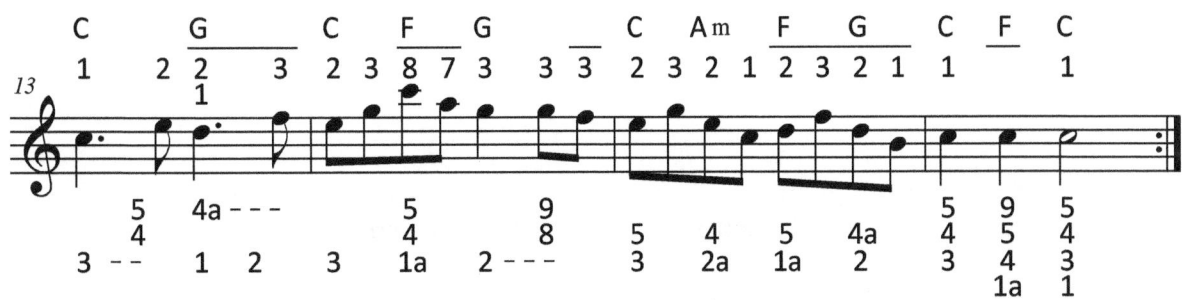

From the Ashley Hutchings CD "Son of Morris On"

Black Joker
(Bledington)

Buttons played

traditional English, as played by John Watcham

From the Shirley Collins LP "Amaranth"

Cuckoo's Nest
(Sherborne)

Buttons played

traditional English, as played by John Watcham

From the CD "Anglo International"

Lumps of Plum Pudding
(Bledington)

Buttons played

traditional English, as played by John Watcham

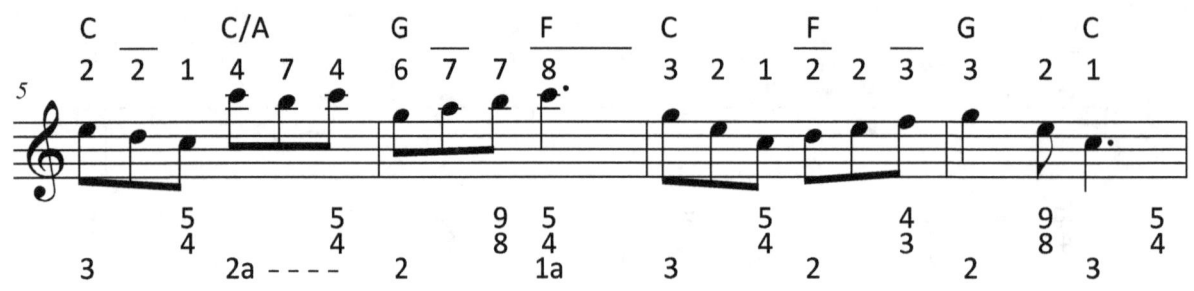

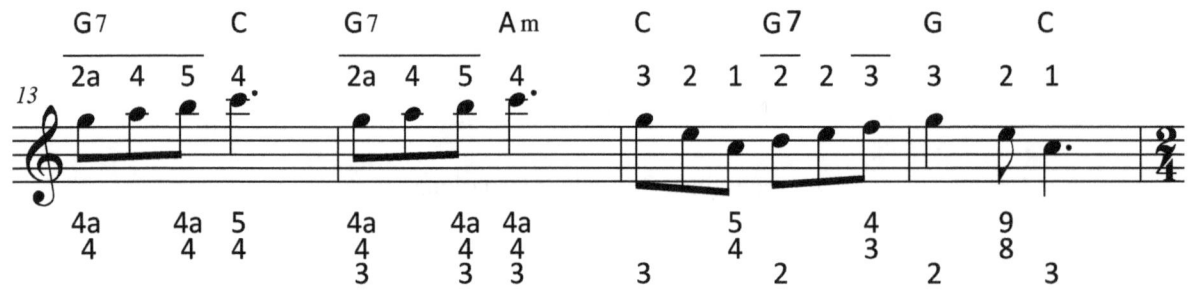

Lumps of Plum Pudding (cont.)

From the Shirley Collins LP "Adieu to Old England"

Fieldtown Processional
(AABA)

Buttons played

 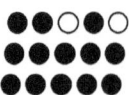  

traditional English, as played by John Watcham

From the Ashley Hutchings CD "Son of Morris On"

POP, BLUES & CLASSICAL MUSIC

Although this tutor is mainly focused on traditional British and American folk music, with some effort the Anglo can, in spite of its inherent limitations, also be persuaded to play classical, blues and popular music. Here are some tunes for the more advanced player showing what is possible on this little 30-button box.

St. James Infirmary
Who would have thought a push-pull concertina could be so bluesy and soulful? Harry Scurfield channels the moody streets of New Orleans with this arrangement of a song that originated somewhere back in 18th century England. To play it like Harry does, play it a little differently every time, often with different push/pull, and with variant notes and phrasing.

Poor Orphan
Another sad song, this one from the pen of Robert Schumann who called it "Armes Waisenkind" which means "Poor Orphan". From the playing of Marien Lina.

Trumpet Tune in D
Mistakenly attributed to Henry Purcell for many years, this majestic tune was in fact written in 1699 by Jeremiah Clarke for the semi-opera "The Island Princess". It was originally called "Second Act Tune", however, it is more commonly known today as "Trumpet Tune in D".

The Song from Moulin Rouge
What a beautiful melody, written by Georges Auric and lip-synched by the one and only Zsa Zsa Gabor in the 1952 film "Moulin Rouge" directed by John Huston. This arrangement was inspired by the brilliant melodeon playing of Chris Parkinson.

Over the Rainbow
One of the greatest movie songs of all time, this Academy Award winner was written by Harold Arlen and Yip Harburg for the 1939 film classic "The Wizard of Oz", to be sung by a very young and very talented Judy Garland.

Star Spangled Banner
Here's a rousing patriotic tune, but it's not the one that is commonly associated with Francis Scott Key's 1814 poem "The Defence of Fort McHenry". Instead of the English drinking song melody composed by John Stafford Smith in the 1770's called "The Anacreontic Song", the tune here is an American one written by New York musician James Hewitt and first published in 1817. The original left hand accompaniment as written by Mr. Hewitt is included to show the timing as well as the concessions that sometimes have to be made when adapting printed music to the Anglo concertina. Transposed here to the key of C from the original key of G.

In Plenty and In Time of Need
With a tune written in the early 1960's by C. Van Roland Edwards and with words by Irving Burgie, this stirring march is the national anthem of the Caribbean island of Barbados.

Pomp and Circumstance (Land of Hope and Glory)
A fitting end to this tutor, like the Last Night of the Proms. If you've managed to make it this far, congratulations Graduate! The Royal Albert Hall awaits...

St James Infirmary

Buttons played

traditional American, as played by Harry Scurfield

From the CD "Anglo International"
Arranged for concertina by Harry Scurfield

Poor Orphan
(Armes Waisenkind, Op. 68/6)

Buttons played

Robert Schumann, arranged for concertina by Marien Lina

Anglo Concertina in the Harmonic Style

Trumpet Tune in D

Jeremiah Clarke, 1699

Arranged for concertina by Gary Coover

The Song from Moulin Rouge

Buttons played

 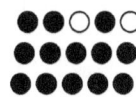  

Music by Georges Auric
Arranged for Anglo concertina by Gary Coover

Copyright © 1953 (Renewed 1981) SCREEN GEMS-EMI MUSIC INC.
This arrangement © 2013 SCREEN GEMS-EMI MUSIC INC.
All Rights Reserved. International Copyright Secured. Used by Permission.
Reprinted by Permission of Hal Leonard Corporation

Anglo Concertina in the Harmonic Style

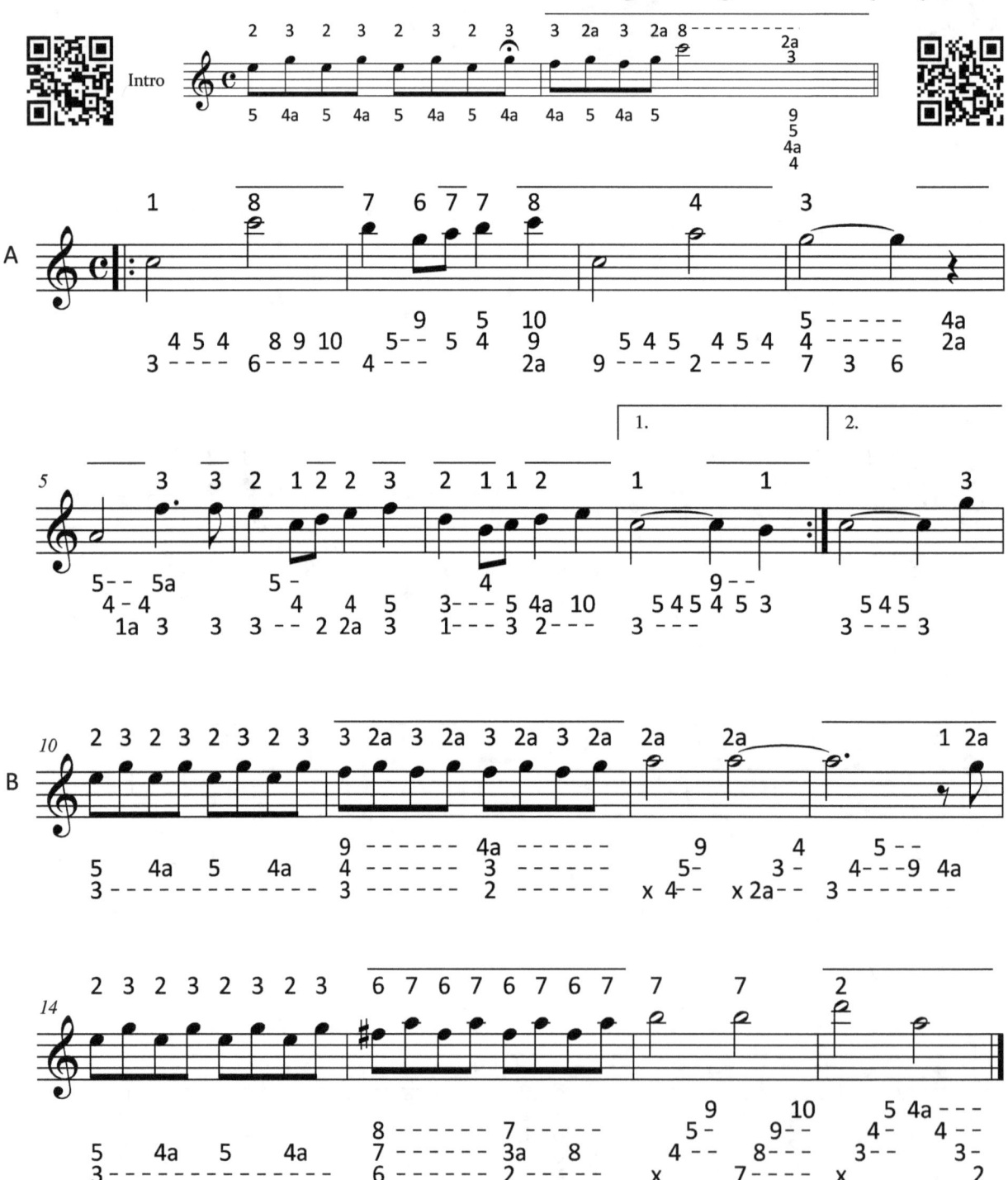

The Star Spangled Banner

James Hewitt

Anglo Concertina in the Harmonic Style

The Star Spangled Banner (cont.)

The Star Spangled Banner (cont.)

Arranged for concertina by Gary Coover

In Plenty and In Time of Need
(Barbados National Anthem)

Buttons played

C. Van Roland Edwards & Irving Burgie

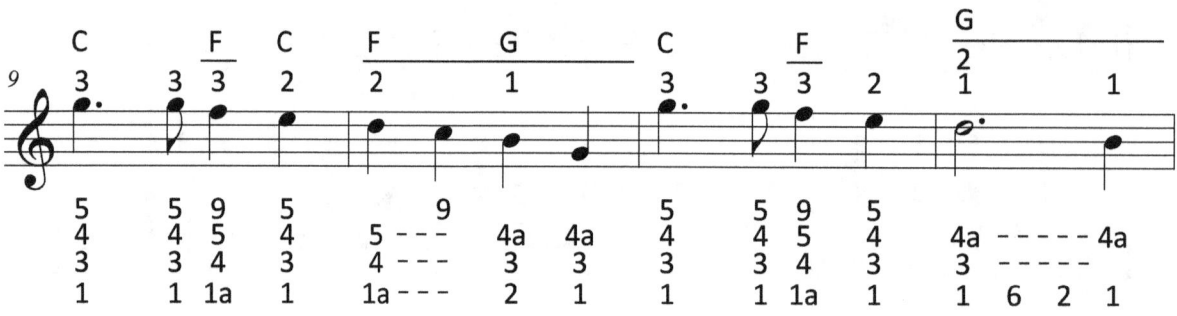

In Plenty and In Time of Need (cont.)

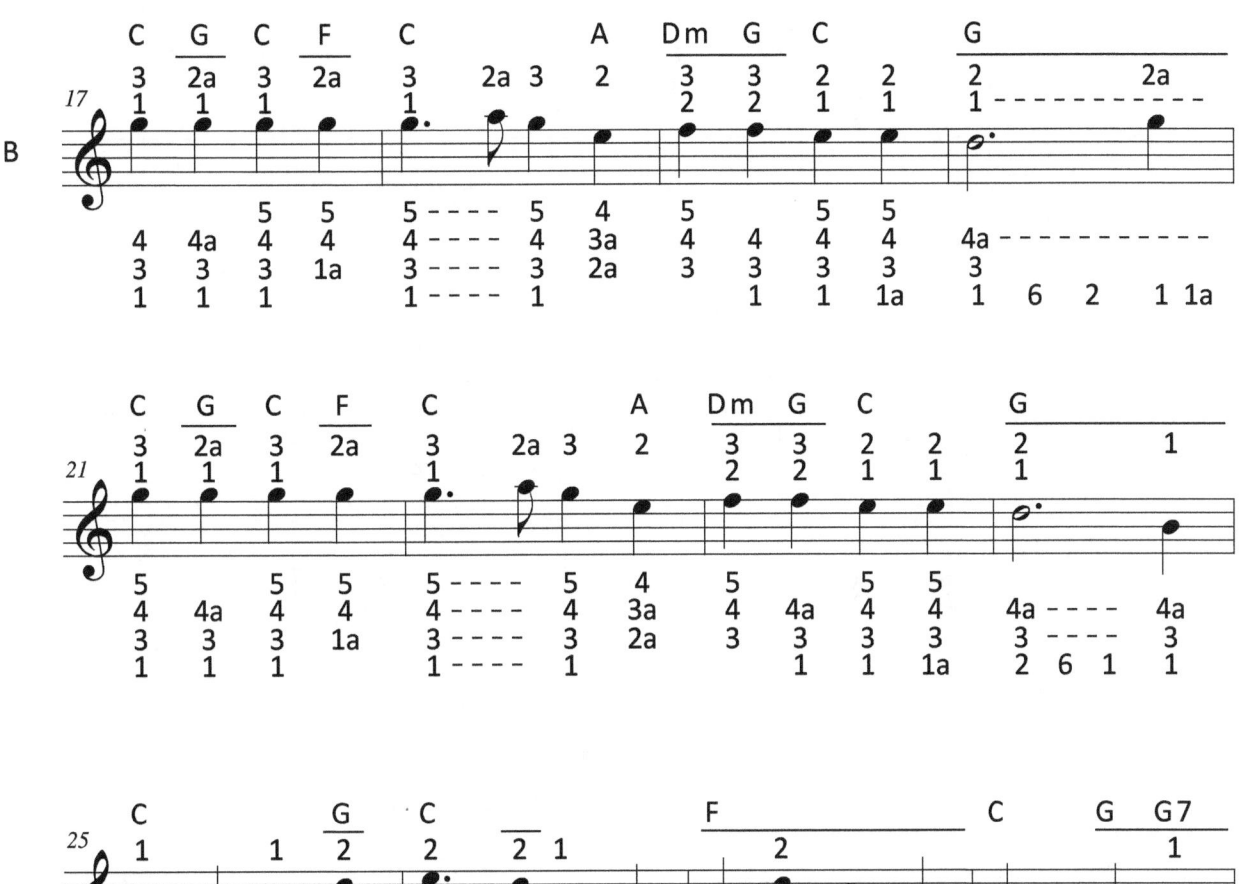

Arranged for concertina by Gary Coover

Pomp and Circumstance
(Land of Hope and Glory)

Sir Edward Elgar

Arranged for concertina by Gary Coover

ALPHABETICAL LIST OF TUNES

Accordion Tune	82
Adieu My Lovely Nancy	81
Ash Grove	39
Auld Lang Syne	33
Beaver, The	27
Burchard's Hornpipe	55,56,57,58,59
Black Joker	90
Bobbing Joe	38
Brides March	74
Charabanc Schottische	67
Country Gardens	44
Country Gardens (Kimber)	63
Cuckoo's Nest	91
Eastwell Park	87
Elk River Blues	72
Fair Play	65
Fieldtown Processional	94
Fly Around My Pretty Little Miss	71
For Ireland I'd Not Tell Her Name	48
Fruits & Flowers	52
Greensleeves	53
Hanged I Shall Be	68
Hard Times Come Again No More	30
Herrington Hall	34
In Plenty and In Time of Need	104
Kennington Jig	60,61
King George III's Minuet	66
Leaping Jack	37
Lumps of Plum Pudding	92
Michael Turner's Waltz	42,43
Minstrel Boy, The	54
Monck's March	89
Moon Knows My Heart, The	45
Moulin Rouge, The Song from	99
Ned of the Hill	26
New Rigged Ship	75
Newcastle	46
Nutting Girl	76
Nymph	79
Oh! Susanna	20,21,22,23
Old & Lost Hornpipe	50
Old Molly Oxford	86
Over the Rainbow	100
Packington's Pound	85
Parson's Farewell	40,41
Petal of Spice	69
Pomp & Circumstance	106
Poor Orphan (Armes Waisenkind)	97
Rigs of Marlow	32
Shepherd's Hey	24,25
St. James Infirmary	96
Star Spangled Banner (Hewitt)	101
Swaggering Boney	84
Sweet Sorrow	80
Trumpet Tune in D (Clarke)	98
Waltz Across Texas	28
Will Kipper's Waltz	47
Winster Processional	36
You Are All I Have	35
Young Collins	29

THE AUTHOR

Gary Coover has enjoyed and played traditional British Isles folk music for many years ever since stumbling upon the music of Steeleye Span and the "Morris On" and "Son of Morris On" LP's while in college.

His first concertina was a dusty 20-button Bastari Anglo that had lain neglected for some time in a local music shop. Quickly frustrated with its limitations and mediocre quality, he switched to Wheatstone English concertina, Jeffries Duet concertina and Hohner D/G melodeon.

In recent years he returned to the Anglo and now plays a 30-button C/G concertina made by his longtime friend Harold Herrington.

For over 15 years Gary hosted and produced the popular "Shepherd's Hey" radio program of British Isles traditional music on KPFT FM-90.1 in Houston, Texas. The lead-in music for the show was the Upton-on-Severn Stick Dance tune played by John Watcham on Anglo concertina from the Ashley Hutchings album "Rattlebone & Ploughjack".

Gary was a founding band member of The Four Bricks out of Hadrian's Wall where he played concertina, melodeon, keyboards and bass. He was also a founding member of the Men of Houston Morris Dance team. He has played concertina on recordings by Steve Hartz, Simon Spalding, Bonnie Goodrich and The Banded Geckos, and posts concertina videos on YouTube as "angloconc".

ACKNOWLEDGMENTS

A special thanks to all the concertina players included in this book whose music has brought so much enjoyment to so many. This book is but a small sampling of the wonderful music they and others have created on this squeezy little push-me-pull-you Anglo-Celtic air compressor officially called a "30-Button Anglo-German Diatonic Chromatic Concertina". A very special thanks to those who have so graciously permitted their tunes and arrangements to be included in this book.

Also a big thank you goes out to all the attendees from my workshop at the 2012 Old Palestine Concertina Weekend in Palestine, Texas, who agreed to put a draft version of this tutor to rigorous test. My reward will be hearing tunes played by them for many years to come.

For more information on the Anglo concertina, please check out the recordings and books mentioned in this tutor, as well as these valuable resources:

www.concertina.net
www.concertina.com

Other concertina books you might enjoy by Gary Coover: "Christmas Concertina"
"Civil War Concertina"
"Easy Anglo 1-2-3"

Recordings of most of the tunes in this book can be found on the "anglotutor" playlist at
www.youtube.com/angloconc